I WILL MAKE IT
HAPPEN
A GUIDE FOR ACTIONS

I WILL MAKE IT HAPPEN
A GUIDE FOR ACTIONS

RC NATHAN

Notion Press

Old No. 38, New No. 6
McNichols Road, Chetpet
Chennai - 600 031

First Published by Notion Press 2016
Copyright © RC Nathan 2016
All Rights Reserved.

ISBN 978-1-945621-90-1

This book has been published with all efforts taken to make the material error-free after the consent of the author. However, the author and the publisher do not assume and hereby disclaim any liability to any party for any loss, damage, or disruption caused by errors or omissions, whether such errors or omissions result from negligence, accident, or any other cause.

No part of this book may be used, reproduced in any manner whatsoever without written permission from the author, except in the case of brief quotations embodied in critical articles and reviews.

Dedication

The only person who helped make this book happen is my wife Uma. There are two main contributions of hers that I wish to remember here. The two contributions taken together, actually sums up this book.

This book is the total of my experience gained over the last twenty-five years. Each day of this experience wouldn't have been possible if she had not taken care of me and our family. The second contribution is even more significant. I had written these articles over the last three years and circulated them among members of my company of which she is also a part. She took the initiative of compiling all these and independently contacted the publisher to make this happen.

Uma – I dedicate this to you and your faith and love in me.

Contents

Acknowledgements	*xi*
Preface	*xiii*
1. The Message of the Spiral	1
2. Luck Favors Only Those Who Know How to Be Lucky	3
3. The Invisible Companion of the Leader	6
4. We May Not Get a Third Chance	8
5. Anita – My Alter Partner	11
6. Brackets to Control the Spread of Entropy	13
7. Involvement Is Not a Mixture, But a Bond	16
8. The Irreversibility of Commitment	19
9. The Real Power in Power	22
10. People Satisfaction: More than Equal among Equals	24
11. Everything Is Fair in 50:50	27
12. The Three Dimensions of the Approach to Learning	30
13. The Total Management of Management – TMM	32
14. Maybe This Can Be a Rule Instead of an Exception	35
15. Tolerating Ambiguity versus Being Ambiguous	38
16. You Are Worth Only What You Are Capable of Communicating In Any Manner	40
17. Systems Are At the Root of Successful Delegation	42
18. Waste Management Is the Solution for Productivity Improvement	44
19. Remove the Short Cut from the Shortest Route	46
20. If There Is No Problem, Can We Create One?	48
21. The Voice of a Quality Manual	51
22. Sequencing the Sequence	54

23.	The Evolution of Targets	56
24.	The Fitness for Understanding Quality	59
25.	The Twin Pillars of APQP	61
26.	Action and Reaction Should Be Nearly Equal and Truly Reciprocal	63
27.	The Glory of the Pareto	66
28.	The Art of Reading	69
29.	I Want To Be A Good and Valuable Friend	72
30.	Speed versus Acceleration	74
31.	Punctuality Can Be A Teacher, Too!	76
32.	The View from the Wrong Side of the Mean	79
33.	The Understanding of Long-Term Focus	82
34.	The Almighty Flow	85
35.	The Paradox of an Optimist	88
36.	The Matrix of an Opportunity	91
37.	The Principle of Uncertainty – A Little Flexibly Interpreted	94
38.	Detergent Cleaning	97
39.	What Is Your Story?	99
40.	Motivation – The Process of Transferring Energy	102
41.	Reviews to Transfer Seriousness	104
42.	A Key Characteristic of the Visionary	106
43.	The Inside Story of the Brackets	108
44.	Predict the Prediction and Lead the Control	111
45.	The First Half Is the Other Half of the Second Half	114
46.	Controlled Production – The Central Focus in ISO 9001	117
47.	The Dynamics of the Circle around Us	120
48.	Can Internal Auditing Be the Most Welcome Process In A Company?	123
49.	My Dear SPC – Please Walk By My Side	126
50.	A System Shall Be Defined, Documented, Implemented, Maintained and Improved	129

51.	The Inherent Music in Variation	133
52.	Shared Vision – The Collective Power of an Organization	135
53.	The Art of Looking – The Intelligent Camera	137
54.	The Art of Receiving and Giving	139
55.	The Story of the Median – The Unsung Hero	142
56.	Business Development – Thy Name Is Success	145
57.	The Curious Case of Abnormality	147
58.	The Non-Linear Understanding of Space – A Learning Perspective	149
59.	Learn To Learn from Everyone and Change At Least One Thing	152
60.	Geometric Progression – The Foundation for a Learning Organization	155
61.	Triggering the Trigger – Converting Helplessness into Control	157
62.	The Warmth and Wisdom of the Black Sheep	160
63.	Manageance – The Vision Centric Dance of the Management	163
64.	The Leadership Challenge – Maybe This Is the Story of Your Company	166
65.	Give Me the Right Speed and I Will Give You the Right Compliance	169
66.	The Deceptive Practice of Becoming God with the Help of Probability	172
67.	My Dear Energy – You Are Useful and Beautiful	175
68.	Compliance Is the Non-Negotiable First Step for Improvement	178
69.	The Shame of Putting the Hands Up and Head Down	182
70.	The Several Faces of One at a Time	185
71.	Good Is Many Times Better Than Best – Absolute versus Relativity – A Perspective	187
72.	People Who Cannot Stand On Their Own Legs Deserve neither a Standing nor Legs	189
73.	What Is Fundamentally Wrong Need Not Go Further Wrong	191
74.	Calmness Can Defeat Anything	194
75.	How Much Roundness Should A Round Tolerate?	197

■ Contents

76.	The Power of Observation	199
77.	Thus Means the Mean	202
78.	The Infinite Distance in 100 Meters	204
79.	The Opportunity to Serve and Infinite Optimism	207
80.	Kurtosis Presides Over a Flexible Kingdom	209
81.	I Waited A Little More and Still, Nothing Happened	211
82.	Independent Dependence Is Always Better Than Dependent Independence	213
83.	Logarithms – The Profound Process Professor	216
84.	My Daughter Becoming My Mother Is a Necessity	218
85.	The Problem Tells the Solution That It Is the Solution to the Problem	220
86.	Sigma versus Sigma – The Mature Adviser versus the Mature Analyst	223
87.	What We Have Not Understood Is Exactly What We Have To Understand	225
88.	The Difference Between Sharing and Evaluation – The Visible Versus the Invisible	227
89.	Strength Depends On Where the Weakness Lies	230
90.	Can We Frame the Customer?	232
91.	Assignable Causes Are To Be Assigned Intelligently	234
92.	Carpet Bombing	236
93.	Learn To Unlearn. Unlearning Strengthens Our Learning	238
94.	The Teachings of Sine Theta	240
95.	Infinite Optimism Is the Only Antidote for Eternal Uncertainty	242
96.	"Maegha Sandesham" – The Message of the Clouds	244
97.	I Am It	246
98.	Fighting the Process Civil War through Good Governance	248
99.	Heights and Distances – The Depths of Influence	251
100.	The Anamalous Behavior of the Result of Expectations	254

Acknowledgements

There is no human being who has survived and succeeded alone. I am fortunate to have had a lot of people who have contributed to my work and all that I have achieved.

My family comes first in my life. They never interfered in my Consulting Career and took keen interest in knowing and supporting all that I did. I must thank my wife Uma and children, Archana and Rahul.

My special thanks go to my Co-Director Mr V Venkatasubramanian and Guide, Mr Sankaran, who read every article of mine and gave me their views, appreciation or areas that lacked clarity.

I will fail in my duty if I don't thank all my colleagues in NNCPL – past and present, as they were, in a way, the reason for my writing these articles. I wanted them to make a difference in what they did in their lives.

I wish to thank all my teachers, clients, suppliers, associates and competitors for giving me the chance to experience the world of business by allowing me to learn through their businesses.

As always, I would not have been in this field without the support of Mr S N Subramanian and Late Mr P N Arumugam who encouraged me to get into business.

I am sure I would have missed someone very important or special. But I know that they will exercise their right on me by silently acknowledging that it is impossible to remember everyone on paper but surely they are all in my heart.

Preface

My consulting career spanned over twenty-five years and about 2,000 companies and in seven countries. I had the chance to meet many types of Management Professionals and at all levels. If I were to express in a few words what constituted a common thread among all these, it would be the following:

- Reaching their level is essential especially when we have to explain complex ideas
- Communication should be straight forward and touch their heart
- They should be able to relate what we communicate to their daily lives and also easy to recall what we tell them, whenever necessary
- Finally, they should be motivated to use the idea as they see its relevance

Most of what I have written in this book is ideas which I have shared with over 1,000 people in training and during one-on-one discussions. It has taken years for me to polish and modify these ideas to suit different levels of management.

One day, it dawned upon me that I will not do justice if I don't share this with my own consultants in my company. What started as an act of internal communication, later, took the shape of systematic communication with a lot of people whom I have neither met nor will I probably ever meet.

This started as a weekly communication for three years and I took care to compile this set of 100 articles for all of you to read.

By reading this book, you are also part of my experience and extended family and I hope to make a small difference somewhere in your life, too.

■ Preface

Nobody is perfect and no experience is THE BE ALL AND END ALL of life. Some of these could be specific to situations. I am sure that all of you have the experience to draw the essence of the message and then deploy it as appropriate.

Happy and useful reading! I assure you that you will not regret the time spent…..

The Message of the Spiral

I hope all of you have heard about the Circle and the Spiral and also know what they look like.

In life, too, we all go round and round. This means, that wherever we go, we come back to a point. When we apply this philosophy to the Circle and Spiral, you get a new and useful approach to life and learning.

If we use the Circle model, we come back to the same point and don't learn anything. Life goes on without much of an all-round growth.

But if it is a Spiral model, we come back to the same point, but at a different height – obviously the height must be higher and not lower. When you come to the same point but at a different height, you have learnt something. Also, we have the ability to look down and see how we traveled, what we have learnt in the past, and how we have to manage in the future, to stay at that height or to climb higher heights.

This is not easy.

When you look down, you must look back in a different way than you would have done, if you were there below. This different way is called "maturity" and enables you to look at how different you could have been or how better you could have been. Sometimes, you cannot see everything yourself and you have to rely on people whom you have developed and who are in that position. They are your eyes and ears – provided that you have developed them in such a manner that they can look out for you the way you wish for them to. This is called "people development" and it is an integral part of your growth.

At the same time, while standing on a spot in the spiral, when you look above, you must develop the ability to see how people above look and behave, and project your ability to fit into that role. That is what you call grooming yourself for the future. You also have a once-in-a-lifetime-opportunity to fast forward to a different view and overtake others and move rapidly to the top. This is wisdom and comes from a commitment to think deeply and to apply yourself to the situation.

Learning is everywhere. But if it has a purpose and a model like a Spiral, it is joy.

Enjoy the learning.

Luck Favors Only Those Who Know How to Be Lucky

....

Strange as it may seem, there is a lot of hope when we grasp the fundamental message in this.

Let us make an attempt to define luck from a management perspective.

We have all cribbed when we didn't get what we want and blamed it all on lady luck. "Oh! How unlucky I am!" or "How lucky he or she is!"

For most of us, luck is just an expression to describe a situation after it happens with a motive of justification. For still others, it is a remote hope on which they run their daily lives – like someone who buys a lottery hoping that he will be lucky.

Can we live with the feeling that whenever something unexpected and good happens, we consider ourselves lucky and vice versa? Or do these things happen because of destiny? Or, is there something we can do to make ourselves lucky?

Whenever I have looked at Management, I have always believed that we are here to Make Things Happen and not Watch Things Happen. From a philosophical angle and the point of view of esoteric teachings, what should happen will happen. But unfortunately – even if it is true – we cannot live with that thinking and we need to do something to keep our efforts meaningful. For example, a marketing team cannot afford to say, "Whatever order has to come to us will surely come and so we do not need to bother too much."

This led me to think deeply and I realized that we can be lucky if we decide to be lucky and learn a few things surrounding this mystery.

I have come to the conclusion that there are three things needed to understand and define luck. The good thing is that we can practice all of these and be lucky instead of waiting for luck.

The first of this is the power of having a deep quest for achieving something. You may call this a goal or objective in life. One should not restrict this to a mere thought, but one has to embrace this desire or objective and immerse oneself in it from head to toe. Our bodies should be fully permeated by this desire to achieve something or become something. We should breathe this desire with passion and fire every day.

The second requirement is to remove all barriers and obstacles in our thought process and approach and open up all our senses to receive the various opportunities that come our way. We will be surprised that there are so many opportunities around us – if only we learn to look! For example, let's say that we are waiting for a friend who is already late and our mind is so pre-occupied by his delay that we fail to notice that there is a guy nearby interested in getting to know us. Eventually, he could have been a good contact for our business. Instead of welcoming such people into our system, we radiate so much repulsion as we are pre-occupied with a certain immediate priority which actually has no long-term beneficial impact. Eventually, we lose an otherwise "lucky" opportunity. This opportunity goes to someone else and we say that the other person was lucky.

The third requirement is to take all that comes our way without ourselves filtering it, and to allow filtering to take place automatically. This will certainly happen as we are deeply involved in what we want and events have a way of falling in place. When we start taking all that comes our way, we learn to connect things and see a big picture which takes us closer to our objective or our goals. We are also able to see which approach is right for us and closer to our goals and desires. Under these circumstances, we will act in the right manner, get the desired benefit and in the eyes of the world, we will be considered "lucky."

So, being lucky is not a random divine benefit but a very hard core positioning.

So, next time we find someone lucky, let us recognize and accept that such people will always be lucky. The person is ready to receive opportunities in any manner as he is primarily clear about what he wants and has opened up all his senses to receive the opportunity and when these two are in place, the third one automatically happens.

Let us change our mindset and create an environment for receiving the opportunities available to us, and around us. It is inevitable that everything good will come our way and even if something apparently not good comes our way, we would have, by then, all the supporting knowledge to see that it had to happen in that manner for the overall good of everyone concerned.

Who can be luckier than all of us, who can make the above happen?

We can all be lucky and luck will always be with us if we know how to be lucky.

Good Luck!

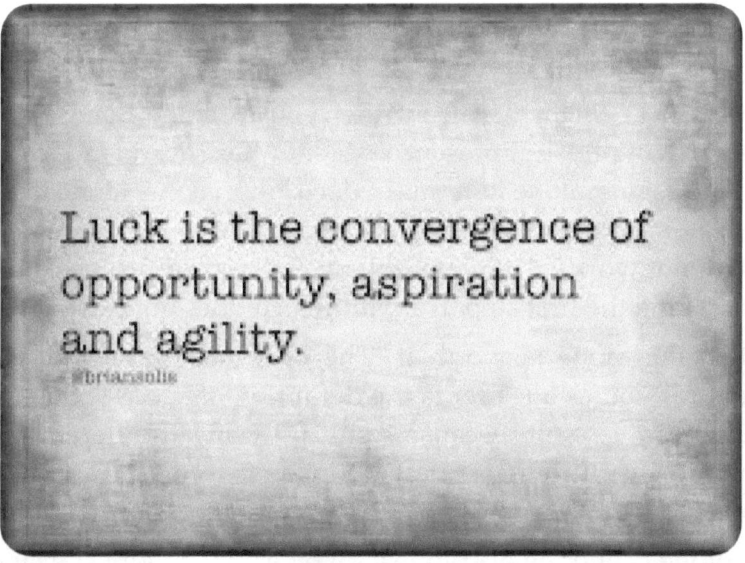

Luck is the convergence of opportunity, aspiration and agility.

— #briansolis

The Invisible Companion of the Leader

There are a few topics which are worth repeating, even if others have spoken about them in various forms and styles. One such topic is that of Leadership.

Be a leader. That means – be at the very front. Obviously, there must be a subject or issue for which you take the leadership position on and the rest of this message must be viewed in this context.

If you are at the very forefront, there is no one in front of you. If there is someone in front of you, then you are not a leader. You are only a follower. This does not mean that followers are not needed. But, a few leaders are very important.

When you are in the very front, then you are alone. Being alone is not only in terms of physical presence. "Alone" has several faces – alone in terms of decisions; alone in terms of decision-making; alone in terms of strategy; alone in terms of facing everyone's comfort zone logic, "I told you it will not work," "Why not follow established process?"; alone in terms of taking the first step in a path which does not exist at that time

But, being alone is worth it. The only necessary and sufficient condition for you as a leader is the definition of success. Success does not only mean a result, because results also mean different things to different people. Success is best defined in terms of approach and emotions.

Everyone cannot be everyone's follower. Many will start with you but in the end, only people with the same views as yours will remain with you. That others choose to leave you does not mean that they are your failures. They are simply not sharing your vision. But, they will eventually find a leader whose vision aligns with theirs, or, they may become leaders themselves.

In the end, it is the collective emotion of the journey and the experience of what happened in the entire process which matters.

No matter what happens, we should spread the message we learn from the leaders we see. This expression of ours goes in the form of vibrations and remains in the environment. This wisdom guides future leaders in an invisible manner and leads them to success.

Even though the leader is alone at the very front, he has the support of the collective learning of several leaders of the past. Only a true leader can recognize and make use of these lessons. Leaders are a cult of their own.

Creating a path where there was none is a great contribution for future generations to follow.

Resolve to become a leader in whatever you do. Take the blessings of the past leaders by soaking in their experiences, which only you can see and experience from this very same environment,

Good luck on being an effective leader!

WE MAY NOT GET A THIRD CHANCE

Management is not in any way special as compared to normal life in as much as both involve people. And people are the same everywhere. There are so many interesting paradoxes with people who have different standards in different situations.

Let us look at one example. Most children during their school days hate going to school, studying for or writing exams, etc. Maybe it has something to do with the manner in which education is being presented to children. I remember when I had finished my school final; there was an incident which did not impact me much at that time.

A close elderly cousin took me for a walk. He spoke in a very friendly manner and treated me like I was a mature boy, and not like I was a kid. Finally, he said, "Look here. You have two choices. One is to enjoy the next five years of your life and struggle for the rest of your life. Alternatively, you struggle for the next five years in your life and enjoy the rest of your life. The choice is yours."

The profundity of this statement always remains. I don't want to discuss what path I chose as it is irrelevant. I don't want to advice anyone on that subject. But, as a management professional, I will relate this to my favorite subject, Statistics, and its impact on Management. Management is always concerned with measurement, so that they can track a measure and control the factors affecting that measure in a favorable manner. In the application of quantitative methodology, three things are important:

1. Management
2. Technology
3. Statistics

Management tells you "what" to measure. Technology tells you "how" to measure and Statistics tells about the result. The result will trigger more Management actions towards improvement.

I will apply the above advice given by my cousin to the definition of a measure, or the Management process. The theory of enjoying or struggling for the first five years has the following parallel. When you decide to define a measure – data is created. You have two choices. Take the easy path and define an Attribute measure which is easy to define, collect and summarize. But the use is very limited. The company is stuck forever with several such attribute measures, which are there solely for convenience.

On the other hand, you can struggle and define a good Variable measure which is very difficult to introduce initially, but the quality of such a measure is so powerful that the company can get rid of several problems as they get good insight about their processes when dealing with variable measures.

I was so amused by this parallel that I start wondering whether human beings have ever grown up. As children, we don't get impacted by the story of struggling in the beginning and the process of enjoying later. I say that we missed the First Chance, by doing that.

Later, as a Management person, the same child, after growing up and reaching a management position, refuses to apply the same logic while taking important decisions about the organization they represent. We are now losing the Second Chance.

That is why I called this a Paradox.

Let us understand this with another example. Many organizations decide to implement ISO 9001 systems. (ISO 9001 is a Quality Assurance Standard published by the International Organization for Standardization – ISO).The same advice of my cousin applies – struggle during the establishment of the system so that we enjoy the benefit of the system later, or take the least struggle to establish a proper system and suffer with the system later.

Have we lost the second chance to learn?

Will we get a third chance?

■ I Will Make It Happen

> THE STRUGGLE YOU FEEL TODAY WILL OFFER THE STRENGTH YOU NEED TOMORROW.
>
> rosssimmonds.com

Anita – My Alter Partner

First, I should start with when I met Anita.

We have heard so many things as lessons during our childhood, but the real power of that learning is realized by us much later in life.

One such learning led me to Anita.

I have learnt the following thing in my childhood: "What you want to do tomorrow, do it today and what you want to do today, do it now." The logical extension of this is, "For what you want to do now, reach a stage where you can say that you have already done it." This is where I met Anita.

"Already done it!" is better than, "will do" or "I am doing it."

From here, Anita evolved.

ANITA means –**A** **N**ice **I**nsight **T**o **A**ction

There is a lot of difference between what we THINK we can do and what we ACTUALLY CAN do. There is a lot of difference between what we ACTUALLY CAN do and what we HAVE DONE. Action is everything and the rest is theory.

From an ACTION perspective, words like – would, could, should, can, may, will, might and so on are not useful. These are all futuristic and hopeful descriptions. Also words like doing, trying, etc. are also not useful as they represent the present situation with a hopeful ending

If we are interested in results, then action is the only necessity. The best way to describe this is using – have done, completed, finished, etc. all of which communicate a definite past and are verifiable for completion, effectiveness, and such else.

Anita should be our partner. A partner who is not emotionally glorifying our presence, but a firm partner who will not settle for anything less than actual action. A partner who will show the way to action – even if it is in smaller steps. At the same time, a partner who will discount all our grand plans and give us credit only for what we have done.

Please don't misinterpret this as a statement which does not add value to planning. Planning is also a form of action. A plan should be so well DONE that it is already implemented while planning. This is only possible when planning is centered on action.

Anita will be infectious as a partner by positively affecting everyone who is around us and thus, creating an environment which breathes action. Anita is not a strict class teacher. But, she is the very essence of success. Anita improves our ability to DO, which is the basis for results.

I once showed our long-term plan to Anita, talking vociferously about what we are going to do. She shut the plan and gave it back to me and said calmly – "Tell me, what you have done this year?"

Brackets to Control the Spread of Entropy

Once again, back to the basics. If your fundamentals are strong, no one can shake you. Fundamentals are the foundations which determine your ability to succeed against all odds – the odds of life and work.

This time, we bring two subjects together – Algebra and Physics. Algebra gave us Brackets and Physics taught us about Entropy – the tendency in the universe to expand and create confusion – left to itself.

Both Brackets and Entropy are related to Control – one controls and the other is to be controlled. Brackets enable us to control and Entropy needs to be controlled to create value. For instance, if you pour water on the ground, entropy ensures that the water spreads uncontrollably till it all vanishes without any value. If the same water is poured into a glass, the boundaries of the glass are the brackets which allow water to be made usable.

Let us now look at a perspective where Algebra supports Physics in the world of Management. Brackets – we learnt a lot about this in Algebra.

Students who love Algebra can remember the supporting power of brackets in solving problems. Students who hate Algebra or mathematics in general, will better remember brackets as the root cause of their mistakes in solving problems.

Nevertheless, let us look at brackets from a different perspective. Brackets allow you to act in a controlled manner and that too, step by step. In a way, we can imagine brackets as a method to keeps things belonging to a family together, and in a gradual manner, allow you to mix with outsiders. This is what we do at home. We have boundaries in physical forms like doors, walls, gates, and such else. We also have invisible boundaries like customs, culture, rules, beliefs, and the like, which allow you to behave in an "accepted" manner. When you wish to explore the outside world, the same bracket allows you to move and mix in a systematic and controlled manner.

If you don't have this control, you end up with confusion – which is entropy. If you allow entropy to take over, there is an uncontrolled spreading leading to a total destruction or a total dilution. Physics teaches us that nature tends towards confusion. Unless there is control, entropy takes over and works against our objectives.

Management is concerned with both of these concepts – Control and Entropy.

The main objective of management is to ensure that value is created – be it in the form of a new initiative to be implemented, or a new project to be taken, a program to be implemented or a market to be acquired, etc. One key requirement is the control of entropy. Putting the right brackets and removing the same in the proper strategic sequence is the art of Management Control. This is precisely the method of generating wealth and value.

In order to achieve its objectives, Management is concerned about several things like organizational change, transfer or promotion of a person, getting a new person into the company, making a change from what has been done always, implementing new technology, getting into a new market segment, and so on. In all these situations, the management will succeed only if they know how to execute actions in a controlled manner. Here, control is similar to putting brackets. When a new person joins, how you bracket the existing people and how you allow interaction with the new person is a typical need. When you are expanding, how do you bracket the existing market so that there is no threat to the existing business?

When a project team is formed and people from different disciplines are inducted, it is essential to apply the brackets in the form of objectives, roles, review, etc. When new ideas are experimented with, we must know how to remove the brackets in terms of changed roles, implementing coordinated actions, time management, etc. Brackets are so powerful that they control the spread of entropy. When brackets are applied and removed in the right sequence, value is created and all the energy is channelized into creating value.

Brackets are not just physical symbols. They are a clear indication of what lies where and for how long. How do things from one area move or interact with other areas, some of these being external? How are comfort zones challenged? How is change introduced, while preserving existing strengths? Let us not get scared of brackets or be cowed down by entropy, but effectively use brackets to control entropy, leading to wealth and value generation.

Involvement Is Not a Mixture, But a Bond

Leadership has many attributes. One attribute is the aspect of working through people. Leaders are not banking on knowledge but their ability to synergize people who have knowledge towards a common and useful objective. A leader should be able to identify the types of people who should be in his team. This should be followed by assembling a good team, based on the needs of the project, and not on democratic principles.

Then, the leader should be able to energize his team by appealing to its "source of inner energy," which is not commercial but basic desire to excel in their sphere of competence. But all these things are just the beginning. The real need for ongoing success of the team is INVOLVEMENT.

I learnt the power of involvement through an experience a few years ago. I was consulting with a company. During one of my visits, I walked in the corridor of the client's office when the Managing Director (MD) came in the opposite direction. The MD passed by and turned around and asked me, "Mr Nathan, is everything okay?" I smiled and said everything was okay, and he walked past me.

But the real story is different. The first lesson I learnt was that the MD had no clue on the progress of the project and he was blissfully ignorant. Nothing was progressing in the project. When the MD asked if everything was okay, I had realized that he was not involved, as he did not even know that nothing was okay.

The second lesson I learnt was that instead of him discussing the issues with me, he treated this as my project and limited his involvement to a passing question in a corridor. His logic might have been that he had hired a consultant and that it was the consultant's duty to take care of the project, and if anything was not okay, the consultant would have to make the effort to discuss it with him. Maybe in a Management Course, this may be passable. But in the eyes of his own people, this will not be acceptable.

Involvement is not asking the status or doing a review. Involvement goes beyond all that. In an organization, people are assigned primary roles. Teams are formed to tackle certain issues which otherwise get ignored. People in a team need to be sure that their time and effort are recognized. At the end of the year, there is due weightage given to time involvement. The best way, rather, the only way this can be achieved, is by sharing time with people. There need not be any contribution. But, there should be genuine and transparent presence and a willingness to share time. Involvement brings openness, trust, a feeling of sharing, friendship which goes beyond organizational hierarchy or roles, a visible approach to cross the line in the interest of the project and so on.

These are chemical reactions and not mere physical mixtures. That is why we say that involvement builds a bond and is not a simple mingling of people that can be separated later. The bond is unique, long-lasting, with mutual respect and is genuinely free of bias or sinister motives. Above all, it is like a child's mind – pure and lovable. Involvement must not be taken as notional, but as a serious attribute which comes close on the heels of commitment. Commitment and involvement are two pillars on which the weight of any organization can stand tall and proud.

■ I Will Make It Happen

The Irreversibility of Commitment

....

Eric Beinhocker author of the book, "The Origin of Wealth," states beautifully that the first step in the creation of wealth is the philosophy of irreversibility. Here, the author is not referring to a physical phenomenon, but rather brilliantly, brings out the fact that the intention, approach and energy are vital for success, which leads to the creation of wealth.

Let us look at what this means.

A group of youngsters came to me, asking for advice on how to go about starting a business. They were all working in decent jobs but the "business bug" had bitten them. As we discussed the matter, it became clear to me that they were not going to succeed, as they were not ready for an irreversible commitment. They wanted to start something without leaving their jobs, so that if the business did not succeed, they would already have their jobs to fall back on.

It is a totally wrong approach. If you keep a reversible option open, then the strength of your forward approach is overshadowed by the comfort of the reversal option. This may seem absurd when compared to the solid arguments which we will have about providing for risk mitigation. Risk mitigation is important, but the forward option should be unquestionable and unbiased. Why should one start a forward option with the comfort of the reversal option? It is a sure case of weakened approach right from the start.

Let us look at classic examples within an organization.

I have interacted with several organizations and there is a common experience I have had with all of them. Most of them have launched improvement programs "several times." I was even witness to a very uncomfortable remark from a member in the audience addressed to his Top Management during the launch of a Total Quality Management

(TQM) initiative. He said, "Sir, we started TQM eight years ago. Again, we started three years ago. Why are we doing it again?"

When we go deeper into the situation, we will realize that the Commitment has been reversed several times. Many a management thinks that launching the program with a consultant and a few initial programs is all that is needed to demonstrate commitment. I have even spoken to a few Chief Executives and they have told me different shades of the following:

a. This year, we will do TQM and next year we will do Customer Relationship Management (CRM)
b. We will start Continuous Improvement in a small way in one division. If we succeed, we can extend it
c. The Continuous Improvement action will be spearheaded by the Quality Head and the others don't have time.

If the killer instinct is absent, you will be killed. If we don't attack the core issue, the core issue will attack you. Only one will survive and it will always be the stronger one. If we go with the singular and irreversible motive of success, we will succeed. All other things are sure to fail, sooner or later.

Look back at your life and check to see if this is true or not. If you realize that this is true, change your approach to an irreversible one. If you don't realize this, you are not ready for anything, yet.

Learn to take irreversible commitment at a conceptual level. Don't commit that you will put a foundry. But commit that you will expand your business. Don't commit that you will employ 1000 people, but commit that you will make people employable. Don't commit that you will launch a continuous improvement program, but commit that you will improve first.

Commitment to your commitment is the need of the hour.

The Irreversibility of Commitment

The Real Power in Power

Swami Vivekananda once said, "Power is strength and life, and weakness is death." The reference was not made to physical power, but rather, the power of the mind. Giving up, losing faith, losing confidence, not attempting, assuming that you will fail, defining success wrongly and underestimating what one can do are all examples of weakness. I am not going in the direction of the mind in this analysis. Instead, I wish to highlight what is already available in our daily environment – either in our personal or official lives. I wish to look at the word POWER and base my argument on it.

The central three letters in POWER are OWE. Yes, we all owe something or the other to someone or everyone who comes into our lives. Likewise, someone or everyone who comes into our lives owes us something. This is mutual. This owing is not like a debt, but rather, more a part of "Give and Take." We owe something or the other to our parents, children, colleagues, customers, suppliers, friends, people we meet and ask for help from, the government, the authorities, and the list goes on.

This owing and being owed are occurrences that keep moving in both directions, several times. In a way, it is like a Printed Circuit Board where the current moves in both forward and reverse directions. In a Printed Circuit Board, this movement of current is not a liability, but the very purpose of delivering value output. So, it is a connection in life. On either side of OWE, we have P and R. In my analysis, P refers to People, as we are all dealing with people and the flow of commitment is to People. R stands for Relationships. This continuous flow of what we OWE to people builds a bond, and a relationship. Some last for short time, and some are contractual. Some are more or less permanent. It is up to us to decide what relationships we wish to nurture. The nurturing process is dependent on how much, how frequently and what quality of "owing" we wish to transfer. This is an attitude which we should develop depending on what value we attach to the Relationship.

The real power in POWER comes from how we create the owing process and gradually, build the quality of what we owe, and indirectly, the Relationship. The relationship is the real strength and the power is unlimited. What weakness we have, can be easily compensated by modifying the owe-process so that the people in your Relationship will take care of your weakness. You will also contribute to mitigating someone's weakness. Spend time analyzing yourself, and build a network of "People Relationship," which will ensure that you don't lead a life with the guilt of your weakness.

You see two people together.

They're in a relationship. It's really power that holds those people together. And when the designs of power change, those people will separate and there's nothing they can do in the meantime about it.

Frederick Lenz

People Satisfaction: More than Equal among Equals

The key objective of TQM is to achieve Customer Satisfaction, Supplier Satisfaction, Employee Satisfaction and Stakeholder satisfaction. That is also the true spirit of business. Most companies, for some reason or other, think that Customer Satisfaction is better than equals and focus on the same and many times at the cost of the others. When I read the book "Customer Comes Second," it defeated all my concepts. When I went deeper into the book, I realized a very valuable point made by the author. "You cannot achieve Customer Satisfaction if your Employees are not happy." What a profound statement, isn't it?

When employees don't have an outlet for their anger, what can happen? I read an R K Laxman cartoon which spoke about a Customer Grievance Redressal group within a company. The caption was, "Look. Instead of listening to the complaints of the customer, the group is complaining about the organization to the customer."

I had a near similar experience when I was in a Public Sector Company. I had been to a customer's place with my boss. When some uncomfortable questions were raised by the customer, my boss started on the lines of what R K Laxman mentioned in his cartoon. My boss said, "Sir, you know ours is a Government Company. What better can you expect? There is no policy for recognizing outstanding individuals. Everyone grows in a very procedural and hierarchical manner."

Many of us think that one of the honorable ways of escaping the customer's wrath is to complain about the company and to extricate ourselves. It is about being seen as being the only honorable member and to evoke sympathy with an attitude that suggests: "In spite of all these things, I am somehow delivering!" We forget that we have to act professionally first, and not take things personally. No one is blaming an individual. It is the system or the service which is presented which is being questioned. As we are facing the customer, the customer expects that we must listen to what he has to say, as he has no other channel to communicate his dissatisfaction.

But I have seen more complicated expressions of employee dissatisfaction, which takes many shapes. Some familiar ones are as follows:

- "Going late to a customer's place when on a service contract."
- "Not taking any effort to understand why a customer changes our schedule. Instead, taking the change as an excuse and a root cause attributable to the customer – vindicating ourselves."
- "Not asking money for the service we render. This is a signal to the customer that we don't value the very service we have rendered and feel that it is an obligation to ask for money instead of demanding our due for the service we have delivered."
- "Not maintaining that extra level of communication which throws a blanket of comfort around the customer over and above the call of duty dictated by the contract."
- "Not presenting ourselves in a minimum level of grooming like shaving, wearing an ironed dress, polished shoes etc., - this shows that we are least interested in ourselves which is the strongest indicator of dissatisfaction of the self."

The list can go on. By doing all these things, we are not punishing the company or the customer. We are only creating a negative image of ourselves and showing our arrogance. This will only serve to erase our existence from the minds of the customer or anyone whom we come in contact with. I am saddened when we think that we can all survive alone, and that we will not cross paths with the person we meet, again. There is no perfect organization. It is the people together who can make an organization tick. Let us solve our problems internally, but present a face which builds a beautiful bridge with our customer – who is the sole purpose of our existence.

■ I Will Make It Happen

Everything Is Fair in 50:50

Fifty – Fifty. Not a very uncommon set of words. We have all used it on several occasions. But in different contexts, it conveys very different meanings.

Two friends decide to go for lunch and they say 50:50. This means that they will share the costs of lunch equally. Some people call it 'Going Dutch.' It puts to rest any anxiety or doubts as to who is paying. However, the feeling of satisfaction – after eating – is sometimes dependent on whether the two friends also ate equally. When you agree for 50:50 *a priori* – the amount paid is understood and the amount to eat is assumed.

Whether love for children follows a mathematical concept is beyond the scope of this discussion. I will now attempt to explain it for cogency's sake. But on an emotional plane, mathematics is defeated. If you ask a parent how much they love their two children, the answer is never stated as 50:50 as saying that conveys that their love is divided. The intention is to convey that the two children are loved 100% each, which is mathematically not possible. However, it is 50:50 only as the two 100% adds up to 200%, and one child gets 100%. Hence, it is 50% only.

In the statistical world, it is very comical to do the following. Suppose one is following a sampling plan for inspection and the probability of acceptance is 50%, it is called the level of indifferent quality. If you have the chance of acceptance by following a particular sampling plan as 50%, this is the same as getting a head or a tail by tossing an unbiased coin. So, if you actually follow such a sampling plan, it also means that you need not waste your time doing an inspection. Instead, toss a coin whenever that lot comes and accept it when it is a head and reject it when it is a tail. Although this looks comical to even suggest let alone practice, the truth is the coin tossing is the most economic option.

For a person who is into the dissemination of information, 50:50 suggests efficiency in communication. For example, if there is a group of 80 people and 40 are wearing spectacles, the speaker can say 50% of the people are wearing spectacles and almost invariably the communicator will add the otherwise redundant statement, 50% of the people are not wearing spectacles. This example is relevant for any other percentage combination like 60:40. But the presence of 50:50 gives us an alternative to use the word equal in the sentence, and thus improve the efficiency in usage of words.

In an organizational context, people in marketing make a sales pitch stating that we give our 100% to each customer. Mathematically, this is impossible. The nearest understanding is segmentation, which means a portion of the organization resource will give 100%, assuming that they are dealing only with that customer. If they are dealing with two customers, it actually means that we give 100% while attending to that customer. But all of us assume that the receiver of the communication will understand this and end up piling a lot of emotional words, which are expected to offer a feeling of comfort to the receiver of the communication. There is nothing wrong if we achieve all of the above.

In a different context, this concept is handy in selective deception, or convenient deception. If we are discussing an investment which has a 50:50 chance of success or failure, many times, we resort to selective or convenient deception. If we argue that the investment has a 50% chance of success, we are favorably disposed. If the same is mentioned as 50% chance of failure, it is not favorably disposed. This argument is valid for any percentage combination, but 50% gives it a charm as though we are almost there or we have reached a mid-point already.

All said and done, communication is not always dependent on facts and numbers. It has more to do with the energy level of the communicator and the conviction he or she carries in the concept. As long as we are not cheating or misleading anyone, all is fair in the approach.

Everything Is Fair in 50:50 ■

The Three Dimensions of the Approach to Learning

Many times in life, we do a lot of introspection to evaluate what we have learnt in the past or in the recent past.

To do this better, let me present the three dimensions of the learning process.

Let us start with the first dimension through the following three things:

1. The easiest – what did we learn new in the recent past?
2. The important – what knowledge did we transfer to others?
3. The most valuable – what knowledge did we create, maybe in relation to what work we are doing?

I am sure that some of us would be surprised to realize that we should have done better from this perspective. Now, let us look at the second dimension of knowledge. The same three questions in a more demanding format would look like the following:

1. What did we learn in terms of ABILITY to learn?
2. What did we learn in terms of ABILITY to propagate learning?
3. What did we learn in terms of ABILITY to create knowledge?

It will take some effort to understand the difference between actual learning and the ability to learn. When we introspect here, some of us will be left behind, even further. Lastly, we look at the third dimension – which adds the TIME element

1. Rate of learning
2. Rate of propagating knowledge
3. Rate of creating knowledge

In this competitive world, the rate of whatever we do is crucial to either becoming a leader or remaining as a leader.

The Three Dimensions of the Approach to Learning

Electric Scrubbing

The Total Management of Management – TMM

In the competitive modern world, all of us have our roots in the field of Quality. We are very conversant with Inspection, Quality Control, Quality Assurance, Quality Improvement, Quality Engineering, and the like. The ultimate destination, as far as we see the prescription in the literature, is TQM, or Total Quality Management.

Yet, when you see the popularity of TQM, it is hardly noticeable, though there are so many models like EFQM (EUROPEAN FOUNDATION FOR QUALITY MANAGEMENT), Deming, Model etc.

Once, I tried to explain TQM to a Company CEO (Chief Executive Officer), and he asked me, "Is it Total Management of Quality? Or Total Quality of Management?" Immediately, I realized that there is an ocean of difference when you try to sell this concept. The moment you take the route of Total Management of Quality, there is a tendency to delegate it to the Quality Function. If we say Total Quality of Management, we have a model for the entire company.

Even though we all know that Quality has no meaning without Quantity and Cost, in a normal setting this concept is not very evident or very profound, that it permeates easily.

There are many organizations which are propagating Total Quantity Management and Total Cost Management. These would not be relevant if we understand and accept the true definition of Quality to include Quantity and Cost. Since we are not likely to accept that fact, we will very soon end up with Total People Management, Total Process Management, Total Product Management, Total Service Management, etc.

But let us look at it in a slightly different manner. Between Quality and Quantity – Quantity is easily understood. We can understand ten units of something, but we cannot find an easy equivalent in Quality.

Quantity makes more sense than Quality as a vehicle to launch any improvement program. Also, industry has progressed so much that they are more likely to accept Quantity to include Quality rather than the other way around.

Quantity is what we are all concerned about and if Quality is tagged along it makes prime business understanding. Banks understand, customers understand. Common people understand. Quality is more understood by its absence, and is always taken for granted. Hence, it is conceptually accepted as a fact and has no special value as a campaign.

So, can we adopt Total Quantity Management with implied Quality and Cost and call it Total Management of Management?

Even from an organizational viewpoint, Management of Management is essential and from the view point of Quality. Management should include Quality, Quantity and Cost: the right people, the right number of people and at the right cost.

If these are not managed in relation to the size and value of the business, the company will not be competitive. Just like any organization which focuses on producing the right quantity, right quality and at the right cost, it is equally important for the Management to find its optimum level in terms of Quality, Quantity and Cost.

This is Total Management of Management.

As a first step, we should start talking about QUANTITY MANAGEMENT and drive all our programs accordingly. Even the Quality Systems should be driven keeping Quantity in mind. I am sure that we will get a wider acceptance.

Find your own comfort zone in this concept.

■ I Will Make It Happen

Maybe This Can Be a Rule Instead of an Exception

This concept is just a figment of imagination, realized properly can lead to very responsible thinking from a huge base of entrepreneurs falling under the category of Suppliers.

I will start with a narration which is close to my heart of a real-life incident that took place several years ago.

I got a call from a customer in Delhi stating that he had a serious complaint on the performance and behavior of one of our consultants. It was a very early stage in my career and I was very disturbed and angry. I took the next available flight and went to meet the customer. I was very apologetic with the customer. I said, "Sir. I am very sorry that you are dissatisfied with us and our service. I wish to make things right and hence, I am here personally."

What he told me was a shock to me, and later, shaped my entire faith in the customer-supplier relationship.

The customer said, "Mr Nathan. Please don't feel sorry. I will feel sad, if you feel sorry. We love your company and your spirit of business. We wanted to ensure that no one finds this problem and that no one forms a bad opinion of your company. Please don't take this as a complaint. It is for ensuring that you have no such problems again with anyone. I don't want any negative happening to your company. I am sure that you will come out of this in such a manner that you become stronger. We want to see your company grow and make a great contribution to India."

This was not just one event. I can remember a few more occasions where the customer was apologetic that he had to complain.

It was then that I realized that Customer Complaint has nothing to do with Customer Satisfaction. Customer Complaint is a very local and one-off event. Whereas Customer Satisfaction is a long-term and organizational issue which depends on what the company stands for and what the motive and vision of the company is.

This brings me to the point of this message. There is no necessity for a customer to be eloquent in praising the supplier, whereas the supplier praising a customer is more of an expected thing, in view of his position as a supplier. Whether it is genuine or not is not relevant. Unless the customer genuinely likes the supplier and he is very happy to do business with the supplier, he need not praise the supplier genuinely.

A very good concept emerges from the above narration. A supplier can position himself above the business and can earn genuine goodwill and consequently gain business support from the customer. It is a bit of exaggeration, but it is possible that a customer feels let down when that particular supplier does not do business with him. No supplier will like to lose a customer. But if a supplier is genuinely positioned above the business and if the customer is controversial, it is possible that a supplier may decide not to do business with the customer.

We have all heard of situations where a company has closed down because there are no customers. It is a very sad situation to be in. Most reasons for such happenings are a lack of competitiveness and the lack of the ability to manage finance. Many times, I have wondered whether the reverse can be a possibility. Can there be a customer to whom no one wishes to supply. It is hard to imagine, but it is distinctly possible only if suppliers become more responsible towards themselves, the society and their customer's customer. This leads to a thinking of the supplier reaching a potential where he is perceived as superior. Please note that the supplier should not act superior. The supplier reaches a position where the customer begins to look smaller.

This position can be only in the domain of softer aspects of business like ethics, environment consciousness, socially responsible, identity with a cause and purpose which is above business and appeals to anyone. However, it is taken for sure that the supplier is unmatched in the fundamentals of quality, service, delivery and cost.

The most significant starting point for a supplier to move in this direction is not to have self-pity and feel that he is only a supplier and hence small. From a Quality view point the supplier has to meet the customer's expectations, but when business is taken to a level where the softer aspects described above become the differentiators in an otherwise level-playing field, the supplier has a big responsibility to lead his organization to change the rules of the game.

Tolerating Ambiguity versus Being Ambiguous

Should we tolerate ambiguity? Does tolerance to ambiguity make you ambiguous? Why do we live in a zone of ambiguity?

These are questions which have always been in my mind when I see ambiguity in the core function of an individual or organization. I can understand ambiguity when we are in no way concerned with the situation where we pass through a brief period like in a party or in a function.

Let us start as follows:

A father tells the child, "You should not tell lies. Always tell the truth." A few minutes later, the phone rings and the father tells the mother, "Take the phone. If it is Sharma, tell him that I am not at home." The child is introduced to ambiguity.

Later, the father tells the child, "You should not cross the road when the traffic signal is red at the pedestrian crossing." Much later, the father and child are returning late at night and the father does not stop at the pedestrian red light. But looks left and right and then crosses the road. The ambiguity in the child rises.

As the child grows, he sees ambiguity all around him. There is a sign "Don't Spit" and that place of full of spit marks. There is a one-way street, but when you have to cross, we look to both sides. We start learning that ambiguity is a way of life and we develop a heavy tolerance for ambiguity.

As we grow up, we stop caring. When someone asks us to be punctual or in college, when we have to submit an assignment, we are already soaking in ambiguity and we have learnt to manage the situation rather than accept the meaning of what the system says.

I am not justifying anything here. But when it comes to any organization where the core business is all about systems and compliance, it is impossible to accept that we all practice ambiguity.

In a meeting, we discuss customers not following systems and saying that they call us only during external audits, and yet, we are internally not capable of even submitting the statements we have to comply with or make reports as per deadlines which we have defined and accepted.

Should we tolerate ambiguity anywhere lest it becomes a part of us? Is it even worth preaching something to others which we are not capable of complying with, internally? Should we commit to anything which we have no intention of complying with? Do we believe the profession which we have chosen?

Questions everywhere! Actually, no answers are needed, because any answer will only be justifications.

What is needed is just action. Send ambiguity to the dustbin.

YOU ARE WORTH ONLY WHAT YOU ARE CAPABLE OF COMMUNICATING IN ANY MANNER

There is so much to learn from daily life. Let me start by narrating an experience. The main point in this experience is that we are caught off-guard many times, and find it awkward to make an impression.

One day, I went to my usual salon for a hair-cut. As I am a regular there, the owner is familiar with me. When my turn came, he greeted me warmly and started the operation. He was in a good mood that day, and started a conversation. It was in the native language, but I am translating for ease of communication.

"Sir. I always wanted to ask you. What do you do? Where are you working? What is your business?"

"I am a Management Consultant and I am in the Consultancy Business." There was a pause. After a few seconds, he started, "That is okay. But what do you do? Like I cut hair, what do you do?"

"I give advice for the management of companies."

Slowly he asked, "I did not understand one thing. What advice will you give?"

"Advice on how to improve sales, how to improve production, how to improve profits and how to improve competence."

"Oh. So many things. Great. Have you run any company on your own? Have you worked in Marketing, Production, finance and all the other fields?" he asked.

"No," I said. "But we look at things independently, which is a useful viewpoint!"

"I thought that these companies hire people who have this knowledge!"

I said, "Yes. Sometimes, it needs people from outside to tell what is wrong as people inside don't see it in the right way!"

We went on like this. After a while, he said, "You must be very special to offer advice which the company people have not learnt or experienced yet! You have not worked in such type of companies. You actually don't do anything! But you are able to tell people and they do everything and succeed. Very nice, Sir!"

There was silence after that. I was wondering why I was not able to explain what business I was in, in a very simple manner. It dawned on me then, that learning to explain things in a simple language is a very important skill for success. Whoever it is, whatever work he does, should be able to speak out about what his strength is. My thoughts were intercepted when he asked, "Oh. You give advice to the management!" After a pause, he asked, "What type of companies? Manufacturing or Service? Big or small?"

I said, "Any type. No restrictions!"

Then he asked, "How about my salon?"

I mumbled something about meeting him later, relieved that this rendezvous was getting over. As I was getting out, he called out to me. "Sir. One favor. If so many people do things because you are telling them, can you do me a favor? My son is in Class 6 and is not studying at all. Can you tell him to study? This should not be difficult for you!"

I decided to take the challenge. At least I – a Management Consultant – wanted to know what I can do.

Systems Are At the Root of Successful Delegation

Our ability to interpret a system properly and relate it to everyday work is very vital. One key topic which every management is concerned about is delegation.

Delegation is not throwing your work on someone. It is not also just getting work done by others so that you can concentrate on better things. Delegation is all about Capability and Organization Building. Everyone has to grow, learn different things, do different things, etc. Likewise, the organization, as it evolves, also has to do different things in line with changing customer expectations.

The best way to grow the organization is to build capability continuously and the best option is delegation.

There is a danger in delegation. I have heard statements like, "People are not good as they were earlier," or "No one wants to learn and they are satisfied with what they are doing," or "They don't think at all, I only have to do all these things as the people are not committed and reliable,", "In our organization , delegation does not work" and so on, several times.

It may be true as a symptom. But is it really true? How are we judging others? Is it by their result or by the process they are adopting. Or to be curt, are we judging people by expecting that they should do what we think? In other words, are we interfering with their thinking process?

One discomfort which can exist with managers when they wish to delegate is the feeling that they have done better, and they wonder if the next person will do it the same way. Arising out of this discomfort is the feeling that the next person will not do the job with the same finesse and thoroughness which managers perceive as their competence. So, they keep judging the other person even while the job is being done with a lens of negativity, so much so, that they have already judged the result negatively even before it is delivered.

How do we overcome this problem logically and systematically? The answer is in the system. A good system is necessary for delegation. A system defines not only the "who" and "what," but also the "how." Since most of us are already involved in the development of the system, we can take care of all our discomfort. A system can capture all the difficult elements and make it simpler to work, so that we can deliver the result quickly and in a cost-effective manner.

What better evidence of success is needed when the different generation of managers can do the work – error-free, quickly and economically? We can improve the system in subsequent generations when newer technologies arrive. The system should not be viewed as paperwork, but rather as an efficient way of doing things which also means that we can practically delegate anything which can be converted into a practicable system.

Let me explain this with an example. I know of days when the concept of Customer Satisfaction was abstract and was only discussed as a concept. With the advent of systems, now it is practically possible to measure Customer Satisfaction in a routine manner and no special skills are needed. I am sure future generations will capture what a customer thinks in a more practicable system and we would have moved into a different domain, which we believe does not exist today.

Throw yourself into the system development with the passion of providing guidance to the management to find a very practical and effective way to delegate.

Waste Management Is the Solution for Productivity Improvement

This is a very short message on the improvement of productivity. Everyone wants this, but sometimes, they do not know where to start and what actually enables improvement.

I recall a wonderful talk by a famous speaker who said, "If you want to improve productivity, work on eliminating waste." Waste is something you can see and start working on and automatically. Productivity Improvement is the result. How true is it?

We can only work on enablers and the result will ensue. If you want profit, you cannot work on profit. You have to work on the enabler, such as service quality or delivery. If you want happiness, you cannot work on happiness but on the enabler – which is doing what you like most. The same is true for productivity. If you want to get more productivity, you should work on waste.

But to work on waste, we should know how to identify waste. Many of us do not have a concept of what waste is. When we are used to a certain lifestyle and environment, we tend to accept what we do and what we see as inherent and resist a change in the situation. This is called a Chronic Problem in the language of Problem-Solving. Waste is anything which can be changed to a better state. Here, "better" is related to the Customer Requirement and the Organizational Requirement.

We should not think of waste from a philosophical angle – in which case, there is no waste. Even if you see stale food, it is input for animals and insects, and by that definition, there is no waste at all. But, when we consider a business segment or a customer segment, then we can identify waste by the definition given above.

Typical examples are related to material, time, error, effort and so on. In all these examples, we can see continuous improvement in the reduction of waste. Instead of looking at spectacular improvements, we can look at incremental improvements daily, and by each of us. The sum total of this is phenomenal.

I remember a good friend of mine, who is a CEO. He used to say, "Let us look at ONE LESS or ONE MORE." His philosophy was that one should keep trying to make do with one less, always. For instance, if a company has 200 people, can we try to work with 199? If we take forty hours to do a job, can we try doing it in thirty-nine? On the other hand, he used to say, if we do seven things a day, can we try to do eight? This looks very simple, motivational and approachable instead of talking of big percentage improvements.

In my opinion, here is a very important key to start our work. Keep trying to increase the numerator and reduce the denominator in whatever quantity is possible and the result is amazing. When this happens every day, and with everyone in an organization, and in all areas, it is TOTAL. We have a culture which is hard to limit, copy or compete. Just as it is in all concepts, it is not "not knowing" which is knowledge, but it is the implementation which requires knowledge. Can we try?

MORE PRODUCTION WITH THE SAME RESOURCES!

Remove the Short Cut from the Shortest Route

Short Cut and Shortest Route. They are two similar sounding phrases, but there is an ocean of a difference between their meanings. The latter is a very sure competitive weapon, and the former is a sure shot to annihilation. Assuming that we are not going to use these words loosely, let us spend some time on these two concepts. The shortest route always signals that we don't do anything that amounts to becoming a waste. This means that we look at finding the best route, which does not sacrifice the intent, but does the task faster. It is economical and yields a lot with optimum efforts. All concepts of waste management, productivity improvement, cycle-time reduction, inventory control, housekeeping – 5S, etc. are covered when one imbibes the shortest route as a matter of philosophy.

On the other hand, a short cut signals not doing the right thing, and not doing what is expected, but rather, taking a one-sided convenience-based route. Almost invariably, short cuts come with a perceived savings for one and some hidden penalty for the other. Perceived savings could involve things like delivery time, reduced weight, reduced purchase costs, and such else, for the first party. But for the second party, maybe more material was consumed, more time was spent, extra cost was incurred and such else. This could have benefited one side. Mostly, it is the supplier or the provider of the service. It almost always penalizes the customer. It is also certain that the overall total cost or time will always be more when we try to take short cuts.

This is what Taguchi's Loss function signifies. "Don't save in the upstream side process, which will lead to a very exponentially increased penalty on the downstream side processes. Instead, spend time and effort in the beginning, so that the overall resource consumption is the best." The concept of TOTAL is lost in much of the current Management wisdom.

Having said so much, it is also wrong to assume that short cuts are always wrong. The concept of a short cut is defined when we already have an existing process or step, and in comparison to that, we are thinking of taking a shorter route. We should not forget Market Segmentation. There are markets which demand different steps. When we take different market segments, the above concept is not valid.

For instance, there is a market for people going to hotels, where the customer wants to sit and relax and dine over time. On the other hand, there are fast food restaurants where the customer is made to do part of the service process, say by taking food to the table. From a dining point of view, the second one is a short cut, but from a market segment view point, it is a customer need. As an overall summary, the concept of continuous improvement is the right approach. Keep improving any process to remove unwanted flesh, and then, we will end up with a shorter process which does not sacrifice the demand of the defined market segment. Once we do this, we should adopt the new process, which is a shorter route as opposed to removing process steps in a short-sighted manner, which will be a short cut.

A shorter process coming out of deep study can be the shortest route but not the other way around.

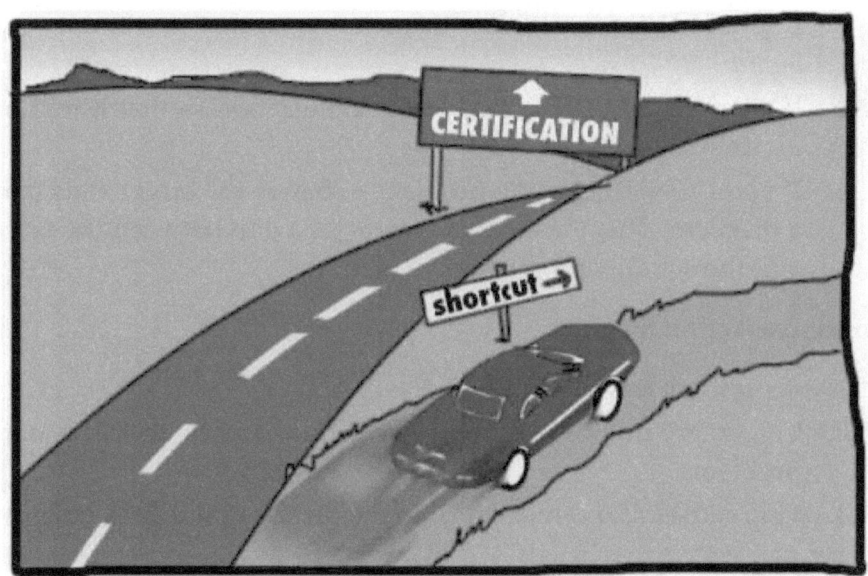

IF THERE IS NO PROBLEM, CAN WE CREATE ONE?

In this piece, we will travel through the world of problem-solving and continuous improvement and base it around the Quality Management System of ISO 9001.

There is good coverage on problem-solving through the clauses of corrective action, preventive action and continuous improvement. I am not sure how much of this is actually translated into operational and working systems in a company.

Let us understand what these concepts, namely, corrective action, preventive action and continuous improvement mean, in common sense,

Corrective action signifies preventing recurrence. Preventive action signifies preventing occurrence. Continuous improvement signifies newer competencies. In a simpler language – we can summarize as follows:

1. If you HAVE a problem – Take action so that it will not recur again
2. If you WILL HAVE a problem – Take action so that it will not occur at all
3. If you DON'T have any problem – change the target and create a problem. This means that we create a gap between the target and the actual, and start taking action.

Corrective Action means:

1. A problem has occurred
2. Causes are not known. If you know the causes, then it is not a problem
3. Find causes and remove it from the root so that it does not grow

4. Horizontally deploy
   5. Institutionalize it in the system

Preventive Action means

   1. Problem has not occurred; hence it is a potential problem
   2. Study sources of problem occurrence by studying and observing data and things. A friend of mine made a list of fifty-six sources of information in a company from where we can look at sources of potential problems
   3. Take action on causes even before the problem occurs
   4. You need a different mindset to deal with potential problems. It is very difficult to convince people who have not seen such problems as they think it will not occur at least in their company
   5. This is a culture to be built in any organization

Continuous Improvement means

   1. We have already achieved the target set for us
   2. We have no problems
   3. Change the target and create a gap
   4. Start the problem-solving process
   5. For changing targets, we need to know the strategy, benchmark, competitiveness, future customer thoughts and such else. A well-informed person is a good resource for setting targets

If we see the last one – Continuous Improvement, it is, in a way, the subject of this discussion.

If you don't have a problem, create one. This is improvement.

I am using a set of words to convey certain principles. Words do not mean anything. If we use all of these in some way or the other, we have achieved the true spirit of Management Control in driving a company towards competitiveness.

Always remember, it is the performance that is recognized. But it is the internal process which has to work to achieve the performance in a sustainable manner. Deming's "Plan-Do-Check-Act" (PDCA) preaches that we should have the ability to define what we want, make a process to achieve it, do as per the process and evaluate and correct

■ I Will Make It Happen

the approach. If we succeed in this, we have built a good system. Call it whatever – QMS (Quality Management System), ISO 9001, ISO TS (Technical Standard) 16949, etc.

The Voice of a Quality Manual

....

(Narrated as though the Quality Manual is talking)

I remembered the day I was born. I came out of the printer. It was a laser printer, and was carefully assembled. A lot of people came to me, touched me, read me, felt me and very carefully put me back into the file. I was taken to the Chief Executive of the company and he welcomed me. He took me in his arms and touched me lovingly. He asked, "Is this the Quality Manual?"

"Yes, Sir!"came the response. "Sir, these are the family members: procedures, templates, etc."

"Great!" said the Chief Executive.

The Chief Executive looked at me thoroughly, lovingly and with respect. In front of a selected group of the elite, including the Consultant who supervised my birth, the Chief Executive baptized me by putting his signature. There was a lot of shaking of hands followed by the word "Congrats!" being said. I am not sure, but I felt that they shared and ate some sweets too, and distributed some to their colleagues

Then, the next days were exactly as my cousin from a different company told me they would be. "You will be the center of attraction! My friend told and that was exactly how it was." Keeping me at the center, the company got certified. It was a recognition which was conferred by people of honor upon the company. The celebration continued and I was in all the important places. I was also shown to a few less fortunate neighbor companies, who did not take the first mover advantage seriously. But the airing I received earlier, slowly decreased. Then, it stopped altogether. I was also tired, and went to sleep

When I woke up, I was in a dark cabinet along with my family, with a lot of heavy weight prisoners in the forms of books. They were all crying. Initially, I refused to accept that I would be forgotten like my fellow books were. But reality dawned on me. I realized that I was going to remain where I was for a long period of time, perhaps forever! How I longed to be with the company and guide them in their working as I was intended to be! But God had willed otherwise.

A few days later, I heard a lot of commotion outside. I quickly realized that the company had a lot of internal rejection. I was hoping that someone would come to me, take me out, refer to me and solve their problems. The Quality Manager was sitting close to me, but he did not even acknowledge my existence. They did a lot of things which was not written in me.

I thought that they did not want to disturb me, as it was only an internal matter. Around the same time, a group of new people joined the company. They were sitting with the Quality Manager. I thought I would be introduced to them and they would be shown my importance and would ask me to be their guide. But no such thing happened. Some of them even looked at me, but that was all they did.

Then there was a big problem. I was sure they would consult me. There was a customer complaint of a big magnitude and I was sure that they would ask me what to do. But I was surprised that they called the consultant who helped my birth. I was now 100% sure that this consultant would bring me out and restore my glory. After all, he had supervised my birth. The consultant sat just a few meters away from me. I waved at him, but he did not even recognize me. Instead, he went on to advising them on things which were contrary to what was put in me, to handle such situations.

That day, I cried as the whole world had left me to die. I remembered the wise words of my cousin from the other company. "You will be a dead piece of paper and left to rot on the shelf. You will be taken out once a year to show to the people of honor that what they certified remained the same – precious but unused!"

We have been gifted to read people's minds. I was surprised when I read the mind of the Quality Manager – the Management Representative also – "Now I have to look for a different job. But this time I will copy this Manual and do the job myself. I don't need this consultant."

I was happy in a way. If there is no value, there is death - either for me, or for the consultant who supervised my birth.

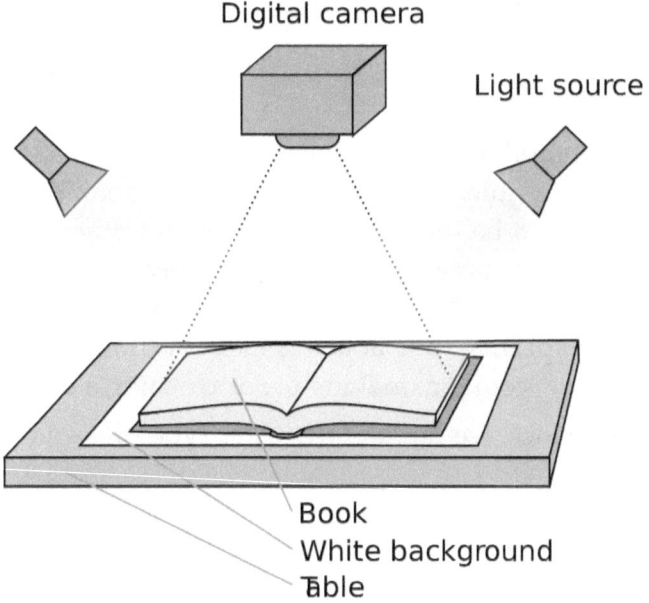

Sequencing the Sequence

We are all familiar with sequence, which refers to a string of steps intended to guide someone to achieve a goal. There are some steps which have to be done one at a time, and others which can be done in parallel. The amazing part of sequence is its contribution in developing technology. Here, technology is not from an engineering or a science perspective, but is being used in broader terms for any activity – cleaning, cooking, making tea or reaching a destination.

At a quick glance, we can identify three types of sequences:

1. The Macro
2. The Micro
3. The Nano

The Macro Sequence is what everyone has as a standard technology. These are available in text books, observations, experiences, and such else. These describe what things are important and need to be done, and in which order they must be done. The Process Approach in the ISO 9000 series also recommends sequence in the development of processes.

On the other end of the spectrum, the Nano Sequence is at the science level – the chemical, biological and physical process which are generally not visible and which lie at the root of all R&D (Research & Development) activities. These things require real subject matter expertise and one has to wait for incubation, before these are viable for any practical use or for business.

The Micro Sequence is what we can contribute in developing. The Micro Sequence is not content with the steps, but deals with key elements like timing, proportions, material mixing, the small steps to and fro like in the making of wafers – taking the chips out of the oil, putting it back and then taking it out and putting it back. This Micro Sequence has to be evolved patiently by experiments, and is a bold departure from established practices. It is done in tiny steps: such as the

Sequencing the Sequence

exploration around the tolerance, the close control of the environment like temperature, humidity, and such else.

This is one reason why borrowed or copied technology does not yield the same results in different places. Even in companies with different locations, the level of performance is not the same for the same technology and for the same product in all locations. We also notice that the performance varies from time to time and from person to person. The usual response to these variations is dismissed in simple terms, by attributing it to culture and people, attitudes and the lack of training.

But the real reason is the short cut that is taken by not focusing on developing the Macro Sequence, into a workable, sustainable and effective Micro Sequence. Even in standards like TS 16949, and the core tools like APQP (Advanced Product Quality Planning) and PPAP (Production Part Approval Process), the real intention is to develop this Micro Sequence and the various documents of PPAP are meant to show evidence of this development and not just documentation to get approval.

Commitment and involvement are two pillars on which our approach to develop such Micro Sequences can be benchmarked. When you observe the working of a person with commitment and involvement, you will notice that they have developed and mastered a unique method which will give results in a sustained manner. You will see such people in your own house, handling cooking, cleaning, management of finance, being punctual, and other similar things.

Don't be content with broad knowledge, but pay attention to the details. It is in the details that real technology lies. There is no book or teacher who can deliver this knowledge. This has to be evolved by sincere efforts which can be realized only when we have commitment and involvement.

The Evolution of Targets

Many times, we don't realize the potential of very simple terms of day-to-day usage till we pause in our tracks to examine them deeply. One such term is "Target." In modern management, this word is most spoken, with a plethora of interpretations, perceptions and misgivings. I can trace five distinct evolutionary phases which I have personally experienced. These are not chronologically arranged but anyone will experience them at any point in life, in this order.

The first phase is what I experienced as the "indifference" phase. This is the phase where targets actually did not make any difference. But targets were there. It generally had no logic except that someone in a position of authority forcefully expressed it. What was actually achieved had nothing to do with the target and there was no impact when the target was changed. It was a matter of fact. It was good to have and was routinely changed when March 31 was passed.

Then, we saw the "Fall-in-line" phase. In this phase, people preferred to put up a drama and always ended up showing that the target had been met. Not meeting the target was deemed improper and somehow, they would work towards meeting the target. If for some reason, the targets were difficult to achieve, then forceful arguments to change the target in the direction of what was achieved was resorted to. No one wanted to be on the wrong side and no one worried about the impact of meeting targets on the overall objectives of the organization.

Then came the era of "stretch" goals where targets were deliberately kept a bit above what was considered as possible. Whether this target was overall optimally right was never examined, except if you say ten, why not twelve or fifteen was the logic. In many ways, this stretch goal was very good as it was a departure from equilibrium thinking and forced people to look at working differently, hard and smart. It was the first step towards competence enhancement and hence was a welcome evolution.

The fourth phase was a very scientific one where the principle of aligning the targets to the overall organization objectives – through the use of techniques like Balanced Score Card was used. It also had the great advantage of buy-in support from the people, as the targets were set through team work. Also, the logic and direction of the target were understood and people could align their work towards the overall requirement with a feeling that they were contributing.

The fifth phase of evolution is the phase of "Dreaming Big" where total revolution in thinking was solicited and organizations set their goals to improve the rate of improvement and go to the leadership position on a fast track. Also, this brought people to think out of the box and look at "never before" ideas to synergize and grow exponentially. Ideas like innovation are sought after in this phase. This will work only if we get the right kind of people who are all thinking and dreaming in a common format with individual deviations which are spectacular to lead the innovation. Further, this phase is sure to improve competence – thinking, planning and executing – as better and never before levels are being sought after.

Ultimately, I am sure that we will go back to the phase closer to the "indifference phase" and I call it the "no difference" phase where the there are no targets and all we want each day is to do better than the previous day, and improve continuously and the results of the various actions are compounded as the basic fabric in the organization is IMPROVEMENT, and Improvement over Improvement. No one can imagine what results can be achieved if everyone in the organization does only one thing in focus – Improvement.

There is no stop and that is truly a learning organization – learning and leading on all fronts.

■ I Will Make It Happen

The Fitness for Understanding Quality

The word Quality and its need have matured totally in today's business. But still, with humility and pride, I take the liberty of sharing some understanding of the definition of Quality, which I have learnt, when I started my career in this field.

The first definition which comes to my mind for Quality is "Fitness for Use" – a definition coined by Joseph Juran. Another equally interesting definition was "Conformance to Specifications," which later was modified to read "Conformance to Requirements." The word requirements is broader and intended to represent the true requirements of the customer and as such, transcends the word "specifications" which sounds more technical and represents only a part of Requirements. When you add "stated and implied" to the word Requirements, we get a much broader and closer understanding of what the customer really wants.

In all these concepts, the word Quality has always related to Customers, so much so, that there is no meaning and understanding of Quality without the Customer in focus. If we take "Fitness for Use," there is no understanding of use without knowing who the user is. Here, the user is the customer and as such, represents the chain – buyer, facilitator, user, the people impacted by the use and so on. If we miss this, then we can get confused by statements like, for traveling to Mysore both Maruti and Benz (Both are Car Manufacturers) can do the same job. So, use is same. Does it mean that both cars are of same quality? This confusion is because we should not decide what USE is, and it is the USER who has to decide that. So, the understanding of quality is relevant only when we see from the view point of the USER.

But, when I wish to present my analysis, I prefer "Fitness for Use" as a better and more powerful definition for Quality than "Conformance to Requirements."

Let us analyze this.

First of all, Fitness is a more powerful word than conformance. Conformance suggests something mild and also looks like a part of the whole issue. What the customer needs is fitness for all their requirements. In fact, conformance is not enough when the ultimate fitness is not achieved. For example, if all the parts are conforming to requirements but still if there is a problem in the assembly, then the purpose is not achieved. Of course, there is a school of thought which says Requirements includes Fitness. So be it. I don't counter it. All I wish to state is that Fitness already conveys what we wish to infer from Conformance.

The word Requirements puts an intermediate step before the user. After all, someone has to specify the Requirements. The ability to define properly should not be lost in the procedural or contractual obligations like a drawing or Purchase Order. There is no one who is perfect. But, the evolution in understanding Quality has to be in the thinking, and should transcend contractual obligations. This is called Quality Leadership. Organizations who are customer focused are those who take pains and invest in resources and competence to go closer to user needs and what fitness is for that user.

Customer focus is a part of the eight principles embedded in the Quality System. This does not mean absorbing all the faults of a customer with smile. This is competence which has to be first acquired deep inside, and then translated into operational processes for practice.

Hail the understanding of Quality!

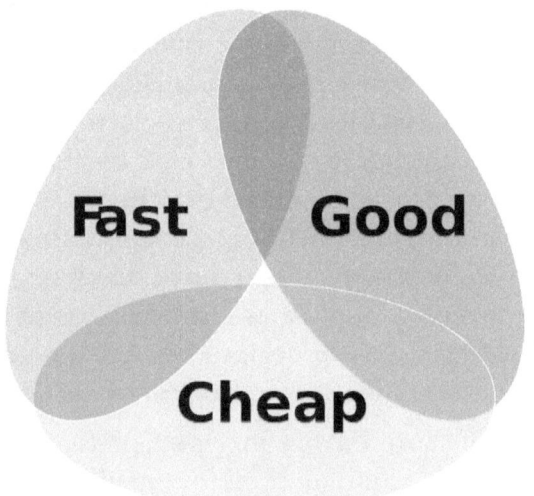

The Twin Pillars of APQP

In a way, we continue with what we discussed in another chapter – on Quality. Having understood the concept of Quality, there is a very great responsibility and competence which is necessary to put the meaning of Quality into a product or service. In whatever manner we interpret, we can broadly classify the next step into two broad categories

1. Quality of Design
2. Quality of Conformance

Quality of design is the first serious responsibility where attitude precedes competence. A good designer is one who is ready to accept and work towards the belief that all problems can be traced to the design – be it the design of the product or service, design of the process or design of the system. It requires tremendous level-headedness to wholeheartedly accept that a designer can do so many things upstream so that the downstream processes and situations are well controlled and not left to human care, destiny, luck or hope. Design Quality consists of three basic needs:

1. The design being able to meet the customer requirements
2. The design being able to be made with existing resources
3. The design being optimal, excellent, innovative and just right to keep the competitiveness strategy

None of the above needs any further elaboration. If at all any explanation is needed, it is only to appeal to the designers that all their knowledge and all the knowledge in this world are not worth a dime if we cannot bend it to meet the above requirements. Once the design is made as per the above philosophy, a bulk of the success is already written down. Next, there comes Quality of Conformance.

We have learnt several times, that Quality of Conformance is not the same as Conformance to Specifications. We have to conform to specifications, no doubt. But how we conform to specifications is the most crucial. We can always conform by producing first, then checking, then rework, then recheck and ultimately the product is fine But, it is not what we are looking for as time and cost are casualties.

We should conform with a process which is genuinely capable of meeting the specifications in a natural and inherent manner without any external intervention like inspection for instance. That is why we say that the Quality of Conformance is the manner in which we conform to specifications – by a process which is inherently capable and can do so in the fastest possible time and at the lowest cost. After all there is no definition of Quality without delivery and cost.

What is the embedded message?

To achieve all these, we have to sharpen the Planning process. This is what we call Quality Planning. You are all invited to read the famous Juran's Book – Quality Planning and Analysis. There is no better place to learn this other than through the TS16949 systems. We have the famous APQP – Advanced Product Quality Planning Process – which is rooted on this philosophy and also gives very valuable and useful tools.

Action and Reaction Should Be Nearly Equal and Truly Reciprocal

I am not a competent physicist. I love this law of Newton's –that action and reaction are equal and opposite. It has created so many wonderful products and we are all benefiting from such products like air travel for instance.

But in my journey in understanding philosophy, I have felt that Newton's law should have some slight modification in the context of business, management and real life, where we have this important necessity to build and manage relationship. In managing relationships, the dynamics are not exactly based on any theory. Many times, it is very irrational – on the face of it. But still, Newton's law is perfectly suited – however, with a few modifications like the following analysis shows.

Let us look at "Equal and Opposite." If equal refers to same content and opposite refers to only direction, it makes negative sense – many times – in a relationship. If a person shouts at you, you cannot give equally back to that person. It only spoils the relationship. It can never be tit-for-tat.

That is why, I propose that equal can be replaced by nearly equal and mathematically "nearly" can be 0 to 100%. (Sometimes, more than 100% as we see later).

Let us start with nearly equal. Love should be 100% equal. When someone shouts in frustration, the nearly equal should be 0% – which is silence. When one is confused or hurt, the nearly can be any % between 0 and 100. We have the flexibility to decide how much content should be in reaction. And opposite should be truly reciprocal. If it is hate, opposite should not be hate. If it is love, the opposite should be love.

If action is based on guilt, reaction should be forgiveness. If action is based on sadness, reaction should be warmth and comfort and so on.

If someone new joins, the above theory can be interpreted to defeat the principle of equilibrium. Even when there is little a new person asks or expects, the organization can go out of the way to make the person comfortable instead of being transactional and responding to what is asked. The same is true when we meet strangers or guests in a city who may hesitate to ask. So, action in the sense of Newton theory is very low but the reaction can be manifold – nearly equal can be more than 100% as well.

The lesson we can learn from this theory is that all of us are susceptible to this theory, and we are sometimes in the Action side, and sometimes in the Reaction side. Both positions require maturity in handling. But, it is much easier to adapt ourselves to this theory, when we are in the Reaction side. It is very futile to React in such a manner that we are actually creating Action to the first person and then the position gets exchanged and muddled.

Globally speaking, this theory is applicable even when we take the position of Reaction. When someone triggers Action, we should first remember that our reaction should be first based on nearly equal and truly reciprocal. Before we actually react, we should apply this theory to take the position of Reaction and then to what we react.

If we genuinely wish to succeed in relationships, we have to learn to think properly. Thinking should be conditioned by the rules of success. The rules of success are seldom self-centered. If we want to succeed, we have to make others succeed as they are the weakest link – constraint – in the chain of human relationship.

There is no success, if the relationships fail. Also, it is not worth succeeding by failing the relationships. After all, what is success if there is no one to share it with?

Action and Reaction Should Be Nearly Equal and Truly Reciprocal

The Glory of the Pareto

Ever since the Pareto Principle was first published by Vilfred Pareto, basically while studying the income distribution, the principle of the Pareto has been a very good friend for systematic problem-solving. The principle states that around 80% of the problems are caused by 20% of the causes. It is a great guide when we study the causes. Immediately, it is a confidence provider to the problem solver as it allows you to focus on a few causes.

More important is the philosophy behind the Pareto Rule. It provides hope that any problem can be solved as what looks very big will eventually be reduced to a few areas. The approach to understand the Pareto Effect has been brought to a very simple calculation and depiction through a Pareto Diagram where the 80% is seen as concentrated towards the Left Side of the Graph. Pareto is now used routinely by most companies and is a very important element in the presentation. Pareto is used at Quality Circle level, Small Group Activity, The cross functional groups, the Quality teams, and so on. I will narrate a point of focus which sometimes gets missed by teams while using the Pareto Principle. I have been a witness to several Pareto Diagrams and have also been a judge at a few conventions. While most of my experience was very good, I also had a few interesting observations to make.

When using the Pareto, we are looking for the vital few and the Pareto Diagram, is only a depiction for easy communication. This fact is lost on a few people. They take it upon themselves to present a Pareto Diagram. I have seen some near Rectangular Pareto Diagrams and the presenter goes ahead with picking the first one at the left hand-side and goes ahead with the problem-solving.

The main point that they miss is that the Pareto Principle is not seen. Instead of going ahead with the analysis, the team has to first accept that there is no Vital Few. When there is no "Vital Few," there is a question that should come up as to whether we believe in the Pareto.

If we believe, our next step should have been to reclassify the X axis and rearrange the data till we see the Pareto. That is the strength of our belief.

It is not just taking a set of X Axis elements, collecting data, arranging in descending order and then taking the cumulative. It is now necessary to regroup till we see the Pareto – after all it is a natural law and it should be somewhere. For example if you are classifying defect wise and don't see a Pareto, then try shift wise, machine wise or anything else, till we see the Pareto Law. It is the philosophy that matters and we have to use data to arrive at a proof of the principle. As Deming says, "Experience without Theory teaches you nothing."

Next time, you see a Pareto Diagram, look for the evidence of the Pareto Principle and not the existence of the diagram. Then guide the presenter to stratify the data and then do the analysis again. Sometimes, it is necessary to collect data in an easy format to judge the Pareto Principle. For instance, you can use the Cause and Effect Diagram as a check sheet. Display the diagram prominently, and whenever we get any information or when we observe a cause happening, put a tally mark in the Cause and Effect Diagram and over a period of time, you will see the Pareto Principle. Remember, the Pareto Principle is a natural law and it does exist. It does not manifest always easily but it is our job to extract it from the data we have Incidentally, this is also a smart way to do problem-solving. Believe in what you are doing and then learn to stratify data properly, divide and rule is an apt principle, and then you will see the glory of the Pareto. Long live the utility of the Pareto Principle.

■ I Will Make It Happen

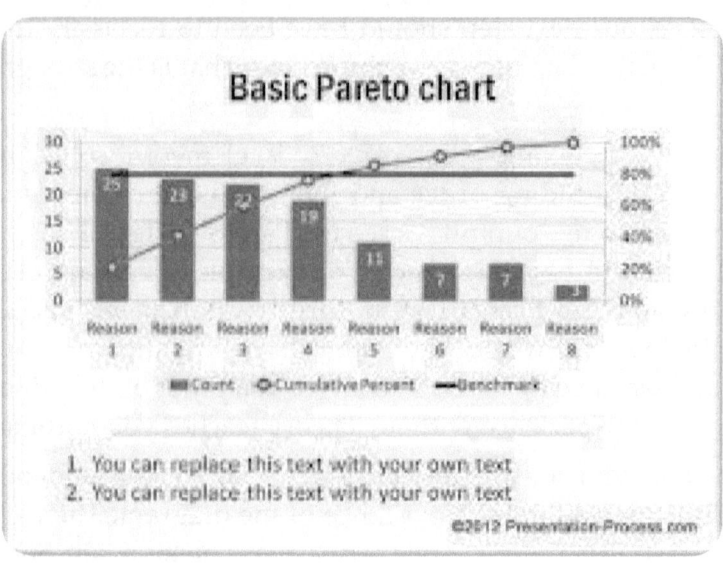

The Art of Reading

Knowledge can be acquired by several means. It depends on the "hunger" for learning and the person's comfort in the medium of acquiring knowledge. People adopt different media. Some people read a lot, some listen to others talk, some observe, some introspect, some discuss with others and so on. Of course, we adopt a basic mode and use all other modes as complements to the basic.

I wish to share what I have learnt from reading as a mode of learning.

How many pages on an average can a person read a day despite his busy routine? Maybe ten? This means, we can read about 300 pages a month which is the standard size of a good text. This means we are capable of reading about twelve books a year. Is this enough? Unfortunately, NOT.

In the English language alone, there are about seventeen lakh books published each year. Even if we remove repetitions, subject interest, cost and availability, we will still be left with a mammoth number which is missed. How, then, can we catch up with gaps in our knowledge? Perhaps people prefer not to bother about reading because of this!

I will share the entire secret that I learnt several years ago, with you, when I attended a program where the faculty was stressing the need for the "Process." The message I took home that day was, "Don't be in a hurry to read. If you wish to adopt reading as a habit, first, learn how to read. If you wish to attend classroom sessions, first learn how to listen and so on."

The process of reading has to be both, efficient and effective. Many times, we achieve only one of this. We read fast without understanding, or, we understand perfectly but end up reading very less. We need to perfect a process first. How do we read fast and with good understanding?.

I do not know how many of you have seen, say, some twenty books on the same subject. If you see several books on the same subject, you will notice that each author has a different style of writing. But, good authors are those who offer a summary of the book in the beginning or end, summary of the chapter in the beginning or the end of a chapter and the summary of a paragraph in the first sentence of each paragraph. If you can spot such books, you can finish reading one book in thirty minutes with a decent understanding of the concept. However, if you wish to read on a particular concept in detail, you can always treat that as an exception. You will find that there are only a handful of authors whose books need to be read, that too, every word. But these are role models or books which you wish to read to transform yourself, or topics for which you wish to soak in the various expressions so that you develop the concept further, or use it for some purpose such as training others.

In as much as the learning process is a combination of efficiency and effectiveness, the writing process is also a similar combination. Finding the right author, the right way of writing and then reading them is the process in which we have to invest time. Once this is done, we are ready to read fast and usefully. You can also finish a few books while standing in the library or in a book shop.

Let us not forget the great principle of PDCA, where PLAN is the most crucial. It is true for a simple process like reading, too. When you rotate PDCA a few times, you have a perfect process for reading as a means of learning. If we can do this for every process we follow, we have a very worthy practice.

The principles embedded in the ISO 9001 series of systems start with the definition of process and then talks about the importance of the same. I hope we are practicing this in our life and career.

The Art of Reading

I Want to Be a Good and Valuable Friend

There have been classic examples of loyalty and friendship in Indian history, starting from Karna and Duryodhana (Important personalities from Mahabharat an epic from India). All of us value true friendship and we begin this journey right from childhood. Statements like "A friend in need is a friend indeed" are not without meaning. It is only people that have experienced such friendships who know the value of it. It is often said that you can share several things with a friend, which perhaps you cannot share with your family. So much so, that we talk of parents being friends to children and spouses being friends to each other, and so on.

I wish to share another angle to the idea of a good friend. Apart from various kinds of support that a friend can provide – financial, physical, psychological, emotional, and such else, there is another area where mutual support is needed. Every human being is born with a certain innate, deep-rooted and unique strength. Then, why are there people who are not as successful as others? Why are some people sidelined? I am not referring to success in terms of position, fame or wealth. Success is realizing what the purpose of your birth means in this world. This is a combination of what one feels internally, and what is given to others.

A good friendship can also be defined as one where friends assist in realizing each other's unique characteristic. You will notice that each of us have very unique strengths. Some can make others comfortable, some can communicate well, some can talk humorously, some can advise with total sincerity, some can make good presentations, some can, by their mere presence carry a discussion successfully and the list goes on. Many times, such uniqueness is lost without any value being realized by anyone.

I Want to Be a Good and Valuable Friend

There are three primary reasons for this failure
1. The person with this unique talent does not even know that his talent is valuable
2. The display of this talent is done as a matter of fact without any proper positioning
3. The environment and timing in which this unique talent is placed is awfully inadequate for the amplification of any value

Now comes the contribution from friendship, which we are discussing here.

A good friend must realize that it is a part of his friendship to assist the other to overcome these three reasons for failure. He must support and guide his friend in realizing his worth. It is also mutual – as the other friend should support the first friend in reciprocating the same. If we start looking at friendship in this light, we will see a new meaning to our daily lives. The process by which this is to be done should be sincere and oriented towards making the other realize and manage their talent and not be short-sighted by offering charity or favors. The long-term strength is inner support and not outside support.

Unfortunately, arithmetic is deceptive – it does not have an answer as to why what is possible in arithmetic can seldom be done practically. For instance, if 50% of us decide to look at the other 50% in this light of support, we have a totally worthy world where humans are in a position which they deserve and in turn, can show God Almighty that they have achieved the superior status that was intended for all of us.

Can we trust the practical side of arithmetic?

Speed versus Acceleration

In my recent visit to Italy, I had the opportunity to travel in the elevator in Milan Airport. I was asking my Italian customer about how he felt when the speed was more. My customer said, "Mr Nathan, no one will notice speed. It is the acceleration or deceleration that will be noticed. You can travel in a plane at 1000 kilometers per hour, or in a car at 120 kilometers per hour, or in a lift at two meters per second. You will not notice anything. But the acceleration and deceleration associated with the start, the end and in-between will always be noticed."

It felt nice to hear this. I was a bit sad that my knowledge of physics was never this practical. But what struck me after this episode is what I want to share with you from a Management point of view.

Every organization has a rhythm and speed. Once it is set and people are used to it, there is no consciousness that we are operating at that speed. This is very profound for me as a Management Consultant. There can be several organizations with differing speeds. Some organizations are very slow to respond to a situation while others are as fast as lightning. In both organizations, the same species of human beings are working. I am sure that human beings are never conscious that they are working at a particular speed and hence have to put in extra effort. It is natural to work at a particular speed. It may take time for a person to adjust to a different speed, such as when one switches positions or organizations. But once it is set, the person works very normally.

What is really painful, though, is the acceleration which actually means the rate of change of speed. When acceleration or deceleration happens, we are caught in a dynamic situation and have to adjust. First of all, we are conscious that some things are changing. This consciousness has to be accepted fully and then mental changes should be made to adjust to the new speed. But it is temporary as the only knowledge we have to gain is not what is happening to us at that moment, but the fact that we have to wait till the new speed is achieved, and then work naturally.

It is only when we start applying counter brakes, usually negative, through conflicting attitudes, that we are confronting at a different speed in a different direction inside the system. This thereby causes damage to ourselves and to others.

In much the same way, let us just go with the organization speed and not be conscious about it. Once in a while, on a planned schedule, use acceleration or deceleration to go to a different level of performance. But then, it is done along with everyone and in an enjoyable manner, instead of dampening the speed by putting the personal accelerator or decelerator when it is not necessary.

In Management language, improvement is change and, hence, has a speed. The rate of improvement is important in order to catch up with the best in class or to become the leader. That is the subject of acceleration. But after acceleration, we need to stabilize. To stabilize does not mean to stop, but to move with constant speed till we decide to change gears again. This is PDCA. Each Plan in the PDCA sets the speed. But once in a while, we change the act very aggressively to change the plan, at a different speed.

Long live the concept of Dr. Deming (A very eminent Quality Teacher)!

Punctuality Can Be a Teacher, Too!

Punctuality is not a new subject. Rather, we are experienced on both sides. Either we have troubled others, or we have been troubled by others in trying to keep up time. Anyway, this piece is not about the necessity of punctuality, but more about what a great teacher Punctuality can be.

There are different types of people. One type is concerned about meeting committed deadlines. Another type is more interested to drift in time and to take life as it comes. Still others are a confused lot, who pretend to be punctual. Let us understand the basics. There is no need to meet anyone at any time. The issue only crops up when we have committed to someone saying that we will meet them at an appointed time, or complete a task at a given point in time. If there was no commitment made, we would be able to escape the obligation of punctuality.

The subject of punctuality becomes interesting only when we commit to someone. Once one has committed to it, there are several factors which we swim with, or against, in trying to be punctual. If we analyze it a bit deeply, we will find that we should have the knowledge and control on the following factors concerning punctuality. Granted that we have committed, we need to know about:

1. Our personal capability to manage time
2. The presence of mind to judge when we begin to slip
3. The presence of mind to trigger alternates to find means to keep up time
4. The sincere communication to everyone concerned at various intervals
5. And a continuous improvement on all of the above

Punctuality Can Be a Teacher, Too!

When we commit, we should know how long it takes for us to get ready to plan or complete a previous task. For instance, after getting up in the morning, some people I know will take forty minutes to get ready, but still refuse to accept this and offer a commitment with a thirty-minute buffer. They do this knowing full well that they are going to fail. We can discuss each aspect in detail. But that is not important at this point.

What is important is the learning that we will get when we decide to commit time to others. We will understand ourselves, our personal capabilities to plan and be ready, our ability to speed up, our attitude to the persons to whom we have committed, the ability to forecast problems and take proactive actions, the timely communication, and the like. I take a parallel from Quality. We say that in Quality, the Quality of Conformance is more important than conformance itself. This means, we have to pay more attention to how we conform to quality. The same rule can be applied here.

It is not being punctual, which is important. But how we are being punctual? That is more important. I have seen a lot of people who strain themselves in trying to be punctual. They don't enjoy the process of being punctual. They treat punctuality as a curse as it affects their person and personal characteristics.

Imagine the following. We have committed to meet someone at 6:00 AM. The previous night's sleep is disturbed. The process of getting ready in the morning is full of tension and anger, the rush to meet the person makes us miss life around us and every minute till we catch up is bordering on curses flung far and wide. Finally, the first few minutes after meeting the person goes in an exchange of sorry with attribution to false reasons and the time taken to be back to normal is full of unwanted misery. Is there any use of being punctual like this?

Let us respect the process behind our commitments. Many others are involved in this process, like our colleagues, family members, and such else. Let us enjoy this process as much as the work we do. Let us improve it to give more enjoyment and fun. Life is not about targets alone, it is also about how we achieve the targets.

At the same time, please be aware of this golden rule – the higher you move in your career or your organizational hierarchy, the more

■ I Will Make It Happen

responsible you have to be towards punctuality. This is because more people are dependent on you and you have no right to waste their time.

The View from the Wrong Side of the Mean

I have always wondered about Points of View. We see many things and make varied interpretations of all that we see. It took a long time for me to accept that points of view and their interpretations depend on many factors such as – where we are located, how far we are from the point of view, the attitude we have at that time, and so on. I wish to share one interpretation now, which bears significance on those who feel low in life.

Mean is a very wonderful summary when there are differences among individual things. For this analysis, let us assume that individual differences are not random – which means that there is a real significant reason for that difference and hence, there is something to learn from such a difference.

Under such a circumstance, it is important to know on which side of the Mean we are. If we are on the beneficial upper side of the Mean, we have definitely achieved something for others to learn from. If we are on the wrong side of the Mean, it is certainly important to have a proper perspective on the view that we are going to have from that position.

There is a natural disadvantage in being on the wrong side of the Mean. There is a feeling of pessimism, lack of self-confidence, frustration on not being better and most importantly, a certain cynicism built on traits like fate, bad luck, destiny, and such else.

Here is an attempt to understand the significance of being on the wrong side of the Mean. A quick round of introspection suggests that the following aspects are noteworthy on this position:

1. How far are we from the Mean?
2. The state of mind in that position, which we can call the attitude
3. The true reason we are in that position

The more we are away from the Mean, the more the despair and lack of hope we feel. This leads to an attitude which can be very negative and cynical. Unfortunately, if these are strongly present, we will never be able to know the true reason why we are in that position and that blindness will strengthen the first two, and then we are in an endless downward loop, taking us into the depths of failure. It is with a strong desire not to go in this direction that the view becomes important.

We should not forget that the same three factors as above are also applicable for those lying on the beneficial side of the Mean. Out of this, the true reason is a very significant knowledge pathway. We can characterize as successful those people on the beneficial side of the Mean. The success could be wealth, knowledge, position in life, inner peace, health and such else depending on what yardstick we are using to measure.

The very fact that someone is successful puts that person on the beneficial side of the Mean. If we view "the position" only from the wrong side of the Mean, there is an obvious chance that we may be cynical. But, if we focus on the true reason why someone is successful, then there is a comfort level as the true reasons are easily understandable, adaptable and implementable. The lack of such knowledge puts factors beyond our control as the reasons for the other person's success like fate, bad luck, etc., and then, we get into a bitter judgment of providence. Further, our eyes become cloudy and we get the feeling that we are further drifting away from the Mean and then the cycle goes on till failure.

On the other hand, the right view is not the position, but the attitude in that position. Those on the wrong side of the mean should not sacrifice their attitude and those on the beneficial side of the Mean should not forget to display the true reason. Why should someone successful share the true reason? We can thus conclude that the only factor of importance is the attitude in any position, which will enable one to SEE or VIEW properly. Then, there is the learning of true reasons. Then, we can safely state that we have started the journey towards success.

Just like nothing succeeds like success, nothing fails like failure.

The View from the Wrong Side of the Mean ■

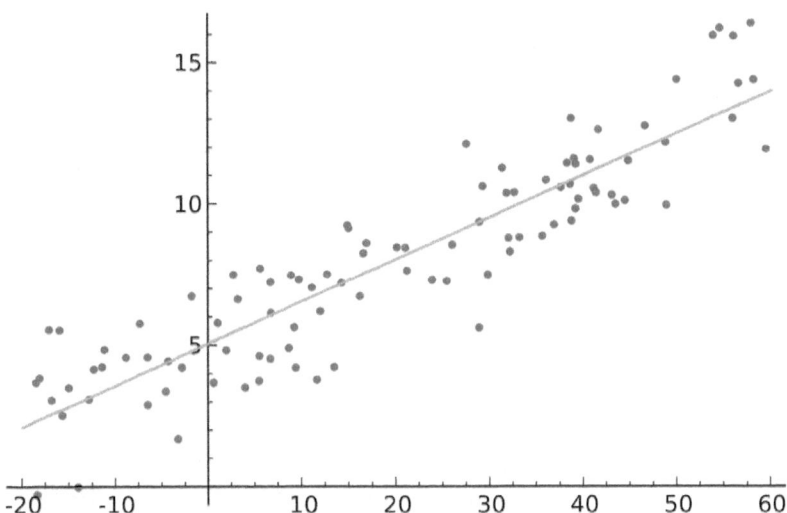

The Understanding of Long-Term Focus

We learn the significance and deeper meaning of certain things much later than when we get introduced to that concept. I wish to share something on one concept: the power of long-term thinking and its related actions.

There has been a lot of teaching towards long-term orientation as opposed to the short-term. Maybe many of us accept long-term – more from a generalist point of view – something long-term has to be good by virtue of the literal meaning of the set of English words.

Let us do some introspection:

Let us assume that a group of friends embark on a journey. Let us assume that it is a short trip. You will almost invariably notice that the initial period will be characterized by highly individualistic behavior. Someone is singing. Someone plans what constitutes fun, differently. Someone wants a particular kind of music, a particular kind of cuisine, etc. There are very high energy levels. Everyone knows that it is a short trip and hence, they can afford to be individualistic. At the end, they all confirm that they had fun.

One never knows.

Since everyone knew that this was a short-term outing, each person did not treat the individualistic behavior as very significant. They would have termed the individualistic behavior as a great team outing concept. Many times, the confirmation of fun is more because the outing has ended. The human mind is not tuned to look at individuals and their behavior deeper when they know that it is a short-term matter. The same is true when we attend a wedding in the family. We don't look beyond the surface as we know that it is a short-term requirement and keep repeating that it was a fun, nice meeting, so and so and so on.

On the other hand, when we embark on a long-term outing, say three months, the thinking conditions itself better as time goes by. The initial period will be filled with high energy and as time goes by, people start looking at each other and start learning to help and receive help. They cooperate better. Even if there are children who initially behave in a very reckless manner, later on, they become more disciplined and ready to cross that extra mile. By the time we are through with that trip, we have found new partnerships and newer knowledge and newer experience which are all going to be with us permanently. It is possible that we learn to see differences in others and learn to accept to live with them.

The long-term approach is characterized by sincerity, commitment to purpose, patience, acceptance, give and take, empathy, and such else. These are qualities that determine long-term success of any organization. Short-term focus is characterized by high energy levels, display of individual talent, experimentation, questioning time tested theories and so on. One cannot dismiss these as insignificant. In fact, these are very good qualities which have to cascade into organizational learning with some sense of continuity.

Continuity can be established only if we think of the long-term. If the same group of friends makes this trip several times a year, there is a different sense of bonding and understanding. This is why it is important to develop the ability to break long-term goals into short-term realistic and related goals and run the organization through a set of cascading projects. By this, we get the benefits of high energy levels of short-term working and the patience and perseverance of long-term focus.

But it is to be realized that the real benefits of short-term energy levels are useful only when we look at the long-term focus. The reverse is not true. A set of short-term projects do not make a long-term focus. The long-term focus comes first. Using it, we create a set of short-term projects and the realization of this takes us towards the long-term goals.

I realized this on a recent trip which I undertook. It was a walk of thirteen kilometers with a group. Initially, the group was not together as a few broke off to take pictures or walk faster and so on. The guide had to stop several times to bring the group together. By the time we finished the first half of the walk, we were a mixed bundle. The last leg of the walk was more in line, closer, more communicative, more assisting the elderly and so on. We took 20% less time in arriving, in comparison to the time we took when we went. Even though we were tired on the return trip, and there was a need to stop more often, the opposite took place and we reached faster and it was a long distance of 6.5 kilometers.

Focus on the long-term and waste is eliminated.

The Almighty Flow

I have always wondered about the flow of power. If there is a pretty good level of potential energy, the flow never stops for anything. Take for instance, water flowing from the mountains all the way to the lower levels and into the sea. There is vibrancy and life in flow. Take a lively place. People are always moving. Traffic is always moving. Likewise, we should see the flow of activities in an organization.

Stagnation is the source of all problems. Take a stagnant pool of water – with the exception of big lakes which is a different eco system. It becomes a breeding ground for insects. It can get contaminated and remain so. It attracts like-minded creatures into it, and then, all of them stagnate. On the other hand, look at the flow of water.

It is beautiful to watch. If it encounters any obstacle like a rock or boulder, it first moves around and continues to flow. When more water flows, it does not give up. Its level rises and it tries to push the rock or boulder – all the time continuing to flow. It tries to locate a force above the Center of Gravity of the rock and tries to push it forward. Even if this fails, it continues to rise and eventually flows over it and submerges the rock and continues on its journey as though nothing has happened.

What a wonderful lesson to learn! What the rock misses is what the water flow gains. The water flow sees different places. It encounters different objects or challenges. It mixes with things which are to its liking and leaves them when they have to separate. It assists smaller and heavier objects and takes them along. It also polishes and makes them perfect. It does not disturb anything that is willing to co-exist.

What the rock or boulder did not try, the water flow tried. It tried to ignore the rock, it tried to push the rock, it tried to break the rock, and eventually left it alone. The water flow is an example of a power which is positive, energetic, purposeful, motivated, having empathy and eventually successful

Can organizations learn anything from this? We are all so gifted, that we can spot any company which is stagnating by looking at the people and the flow of activities. A lively place, buzzing with activity, people moving constantly around and forward – attracts more people. It is impossible to laze around in a busy street, which has people moving at a brisk pace. Likewise, it is impossible to see failure in an organization which is on the move – people moving around and forward and activities proceeding at a pace which is desired.

Such organizations can have a strong influence on people who otherwise would have stagnated. The flow will try to first ignore such people showing them that they will be neglected if they don't change. Later, it moves around them to show that life is better moving. Gradually it will apply pressure on them and try to make them move. If nothing happens, it submerges those laggards and moves on. Nothing can stop an organization on the move – people and activities flowing.

There is something called – making the effort. Instead of neglecting, we should use the power of flow and change ourselves and those who need to change. There is no guarantee that anything will change – except us. But at least this trial will make an impact somewhere. Those sitting on the wall will certainly get swept into the flow. Those who have loose resistance will also be swept into the flow. Those with moderate resistance will eventually be swept into the flow. Finally those with the strongest resistance will get an impact – an awareness, an awakening, a story to learn – but if they decide to remain strongly rooted, then they remain there forever or till the force of nature takes them away.

Another way to interpret this is to have less baggage and be light. Don't carry too many bad memories, too many bad examples, too much of skepticism but instead have a firm interest to live, love, learn and levitate.

The Almighty Flow

The Paradox of an Optimist

We have all heard that variety is the spice of life and what better manifestation of this variety can we see other than in people? We are all part of the population of people and we know how fascinating it is to see the variety among all of us. There are several types of people and each have contributory and successful characteristics and a lifetime of study is not enough even to do a simple comparative analysis.

I talk about one category called the Optimist. It is my favorite. It is easy to identify an optimist. An optimist is a person who sees the positive side of any situation. They are believers in eternal hope and are never tired of life. They always have something to do and work with a great deal of positive energy. Those optimists who are also good communicators, I believe most of them are naturally disposed to be better communicators, have a great ability to carry people along with them and can even influence the life of others. No one will disagree that they will come with a better state of mind after encountering an optimist. Let us not take this too far.

An optimist need not be successful. Being an optimist does not guarantee success. Being an optimist guarantees a very positive approach, a very motivating atmosphere and a natural tendency to find something better to move forward even while facing adversity. It is not overconfidence, but a genuine feeling that success will come which distinguishes the optimist from others. In order to be successful, three qualities are necessary:

1. Being an optimist
2. Being talented
3. Having luck

Earlier, I believed that talent and luck are enough to be successful. Unfortunately, I have seen a lot of talented people who do not see the brighter side of an opportunity. They lack confidence in themselves.

They don't want to try. Unless you try, there is no way to know whether we will succeed and more importantly, whether an opportunity is really an opportunity or just an imaginary perception.

In my opinion, optimism is like a kick-start in racing. The real advantage is for those who try. It is here that the optimist fits well. Being an optimist will ensure that there is a start and an approach with positivity and an atmosphere which is motivating. The optimist can get people together and take them along. But optimism is just one among the three imperatives for success.

If a talented person is an optimist or if an optimist is also talented, then the odds for success have already crossed the half-way mark and gets closer to success. But still, it is not enough. What very few people understand or accept is that the final success is dictated by luck. This does not sound very encouraging, especially for people who have succeeded and who wish to believe that all success is due to their talent. There is enough evidence to show that optimists almost always lose double as compared to normal people. Partly, this is because of their refusal to let go when failure stares in their face.

It is very nice to succeed and to talk about success. But attributing 100% success to 100% talent and being an optimist is wrong. Let us not undermine the effect of luck much as it does not give a feeling of control. At the end, we are all destined to play a role and we should play it well. Let the optimist in us detect and act on any opportunity that exists and remain with our neck firmly above the shoulder and below the head.

Luck is a great factor which influences several things. We know so many people – equally optimistic and talented, who have embarked on many projects. But not all have succeeded. The famous book "Fooled by Randomness" suggests that we should look at how many people started at the same time when we look at the success story of anyone, and then based on the statistics, conclude what factor has really contributed for success. It has been proven that many of the success stories are by a factor called randomness. I don't know what randomness is. Maybe it is another name for luck.

(Here the word Luck is taken on the face value but the reader is invited to see my chapter on Being Lucky for a better insight into Luck).

■ I Will Make It Happen

The Matrix of an Opportunity

GROWTH is essential as there is nothing stagnant in life. We either grow or perish. There is no such thing as maintenance. Also, there is no excitement in linear growth. The way to reach far and wide and explore what life has to offer is through exponential growth. There are very few things which teach us the power of exponential growth and the means to achieve this.

Knowing about the need to grow is not sufficient. We should also know about simple mechanisms which assure us of a solid, near foolproof method which can help us grow – provided we are disciplined enough to understand the mechanism and put it into practice. Again, my favorite subject Mathematics gives me a valuable concept in this regard: the Matrix.

It is only people who have experienced the use of matrices know about this exponential formula. For others, I assure you of the same result provided you start respecting and loving matrices.

A matrix consists of a set of rows and columns. We know about Microsoft Excel. The beauty of the matrix system is its amazing and practically infinite set of row and column interaction cells. If you have ten rows and ten columns, the set of interaction cells is 100 and if you add just one row and one column, the set of interacting cells becomes 121 – the concept of Exponential Opportunity stems from here. From a business point of view, if you have ten customers and ten services, you have 100 opportunities – barring a few in the diagonal. This is an amazing opportunity to explore.

People in marketing can use this concept to either evaluate opportunities for existing services or explore new service opportunities. With a little creativity, we can get into the world of Innovation to outsmart the competition. This is just a two- dimensional approach.

■ I Will Make It Happen

If you can imagine a third dimension, we have a life time of work in front of us. The same concept can be used for operations to judge competence, finance for exploration of best finance option, HR (Human Resources) for evaluating the deployment of manpower and for training and so on.

For a change, let us leave the business arena and look at life. The matrix is a simple method to build relationships. Relationships are the most crucial starting and eternal virtue of life. One can do anything if the right relationships are in place.

Let us use the interaction aspect of the Matrix to build relationships. If you know 100 people and put the 100 people in the rows and the same 100 people in the columns you have 10000 opportunities for building and growing the relationships. The growth element comes when you put yourself between the two people represented in each interacting cell. You can have as many potential possibilities as you can imagine with each interacting cell.

The following are a few possibilities, but they are by no means exhaustive.

1. What you can give or take from one person
2. What you can give or take from the other person
3. What one person can give or take from the other person
4. What you with one person can offer to the other person
5. What you with the other person can offer to the second person
6. What all three can offer to each other
7. What the three of you can offer and thus create another matrix set of opportunities to a fourth person.

The list is endless – limited by your interest, imagination and application.

Life is about Give and Take. You must Give first and then look at Take. In fact pure relationship building is not to look at what you Take but what you Give. What is due to you will automatically come. We are too small to even understand what has come back to us. What we expect is not what is right. What happens is what is right and hence allow things to happen and you will certainly benefit and that is Right.

The fact that you are alive, the fact that you have a lot of people to talk to, the fact that you have a valuable relationship with the people you know, the fact that you concentrate on what the others gain in value and the fact that together you create more nucleus and more several dimensional matrices makes the purpose of life strong and consequently are examples of what has come back to you.

The vision to see through what a network you can create which grows exponentially and on its own is the purpose of creation. Humans have grown that way. All living beings have grown that way. Then why wait for anything better to further the process of relationship building and creation of an exponential set of opportunities to explore life.

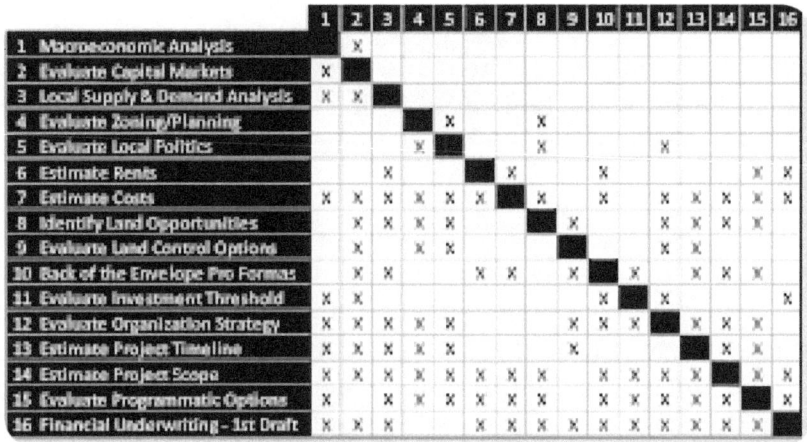

The Principle of Uncertainty – A Little Flexibly Interpreted

I will attempt a technical subject this time –the Principle of Uncertainty. To many, this may look very technical. But once you concentrate, you will find that this is amazingly simple and absolutely profound. I am not referring to the simple probabilistic understanding of uncertainty or the straightforward English meaning of this term. I am drawing the understanding from the Measurement Systems and Calibration domain.

Let us first discuss the technical understanding. We are always interested in measurement and keep measuring different things for different reasons – time, weight, length, quantity, etc. The only requirement here is to know what the truth is, or in technical terms – True Value. But science tells us that there is no such thing as True value and you can never measure anything right.

Why?

You go to a petrol pump and measure the tyre pressure. We put a hose and then read the pressure through a gauge. But while measuring the pressure, you are actually drawing some air from the tyre and consequently what you measure is impacted less by that amount – it may be very small but in principle it is true. So, the actual act of measurement delivers a certain Uncertainty to what is measured. Hence we say that the true value is a concept and no one can measure it. We can only specify a band around the true value which is called Uncertainty. This uncertainty gets transmitted in subsequent measurements and has a cascading effect downstream.

The definition of Uncertainty actually conveys a wonderful philosophy. Instead of trying to find the true value, you specify a small band within which the true value lies. The actual position of true value is irrelevant but the band within which it lies becomes important.

This simple idea throws three important offshoots, which has a very deep impact in Management. The three ideas are

1. There is no tension in trying to find the absolute value but as long as you are in a band, it is fine. This is a trade-off between absolute and rigid to relative and flexible. It is a great motivator for people putting the efforts as they need not be paranoid about getting to a particular target. They have the freedom to explore what the optimum is.
2. It is an economic trade-off. The cost incurred in reducing uncertainty versus the benefits. It is a win-win situation where you adopt the position of "Give some and take some." Interpreting it in a different context, say Marketing, this is a trade-off where you win the contract and also give a feeling to the customer that there is some concession.
3. The principle of uncertainty is propagated to the full stream of activity in the chain which actually can be interpreted as a transmission of the culture – flexibility in approach, no tension in trying to reach an absolute position, an economic trade-off or strategic give and take and a cultural transmission to other levels.

This principle when taken in a Management situation means the following:

1. Have a well-defined target
2. Don't get paranoid but have a flexible and good practical approach
3. Evaluate in such a manner that there is a win-win or give-take
4. Pass the message to others to work without fear of failure
5. Continuously improve the uncertainty to lower levels where you are as close to the truth but at the same time enjoy the journey which is the actual work life

Instead of being uncertain about what you are doing, use uncertainty to move towards certainty, of what you wish to achieve.

■ I Will Make It Happen

Detergent Cleaning

A lot has been written about chemistry and its role in human relations and psychology. The knowledge gained from physics, chemistry and mathematics can be used in a wide variety of situations through proper interpretation. I have attempted a few such interpretations in the past. This time, I wish to share a concept from chemistry, called " Detergent Cleaning," and its relevance to Management. The process has been imagined to convey a message on management.

Detergent Cleaning is the use of a detergent, like soap, to remove dirt. Chemistry describes how the detergent acts on the dirt by first enveloping it and then gradually covering it entirely, and then flushes it out with water, giving the dirt no chance to escape. If you look at this process deeply, you will find the following process steps as significant:

1. Reaching the dirt particle
2. Forming a layer over it
3. Going under the dirt to remove it gently from the base surface
4. Ensure that the base surface is not damaged
5. Enclose the dirt fully and wait for it to be flushed
6. Getting flushed out of the system

It is important to recognize that the base or mother material like the fabric should not get damaged while removing the dirt. This means that we have to use the right concentration of the detergent. If we use physical force, the fabric will get damaged. In a real life Management situation, we find a lot of opportunities where we are left with problems in the organizational fabric: bad attitudes, bad egoistic behavior, poor approach to work, bad human relations and the like, which can all be traced to a few ill-advised people and their concepts. This is the kind of dirt that has to be removed, but without damaging the organization.

Just like in the case of fabric, it is not possible to identify small pockets of dirt. This is also the case in the context of Management. We cannot isolate small pockets of dirt or bad attitudes. Incidentally, very large patches of attitude-related issues can be easily tackled. But, it is the smaller scattered pockets of dirt that eventually build up the cracks in the organization. They are to be tackled systematically. The above six-step process is equally applicable for Management situations. Without using force or overdose of any formula, we need an overall application of programs in the organization. These programs have to born out of a very good heart, a well-planned approach, systematic deployment, allowing sufficient time for the cleaning to take place and then the bad elements are carefully flushed out without anyone getting into any emotional situations. Time is of essence, which means that these programs are to be applied frequently and consequently, the organization purged out of bad elements of behavior. Just like in a fabric, the organization is cleaned, dried and rejuvenated, or rather, reborn.

The key aspect of this concept is timeliness and continuity. Allowing long periods of time to lapse will make the dirt get strongly attached to the fabric. We will be left with no choice but to use brute force or strong detergents. Both approaches damage the fabric irrevocably. The same is true of organizations. Don't arrive at a situation where you have to use huge forces, because good elements are affected and the net result is very bad taste and a fragile organization. Many a time, the organization collapses. It is easy to destroy what is created. But, it takes more effort and perseverance in sustaining the organization. Let us learn from all the associated sciences and improve ourselves, our organization and above all, the legacy we have created.

What Is Your Story?

I am sharing something that we all experience, and this is personal. The irony is that it has to be personal, as otherwise, when we try to communicate with others, it makes no sense to them. That, in turn, dilutes the power of your attachment to yourself. Let us look at the following things. We see a person in the morning and ask him how he is. The person says he is fine. This is at the surface level. But, beneath the surface, there is a story that the person has faced, and many times, their story is irrelevant to us. However, the story is very significant to that person. Let me tell you my story. On Wednesday, May 22, 2015, I traveled to Chennai to meet a German customer.

Whatever may have been destiny's plan for me, I did not get confirmation for my berth on the train. I started by a bus that left at 7:30 AM. When I got into the bus, I told myself that I would sleep on the ride. True to this, I started to relax even before the bus left the Bangalore bus depot. Suddenly, I found a lady aged over sixty-five, waking me up and asking me whether Chennai was the last stop, and if not, what the name of the last stop was. I told her it was Koyambedu (Central Bus Stop in Chennai, India) and she asked me whether there was only one Koyambedu. I convinced her to relax and went to sleep. I don't know how long I slept when she woke me again. She started complaining about her arm having gone numb. We did some first aid, and my irritation in not being able to sleep prevented me from doing this in a compassionate manner. Again, I drifted off to sleep. After some time, she woke me up and asked, "Have we arrived at Koyambedu? "I looked around and found that we were near Vellore. I told her to relax and there was a lot of time ahead of us. By now, I had lost my sleep. When I looked at her, she was sleeping like a baby. Maybe this was destiny. She had to watch me sleep and I had to reciprocate. Finally, we reached Chennai and I told her how to reach her destination. Then, I got down to a welcome blast of hot Chennai air.

■ I Will Make It Happen

    I decided to eat at Murugan Idli (a famous food outlet in Chennai), praying that the lunch section would be open. I reached at 3:00 PM, and was relieved to find that lunch closed at 3:30 PM. But as my bad luck would have it, I had to wait as the rice I had ordered was not ready. I waited, and my irritation increased. Finally, lunch arrived, but it was very hot. Between keeping the appointment and eating well, I sacrificed the latter. With burnt fingers and mouth, I finished lunch and reached Hotel Hyatt for my appointment. After the meeting, I came back to the Chennai heat, crossed Mount Road and started walking slowly, wondering what I should do next. I don't know how it happened, but I slipped on the footpath and fell down on the road. My first reaction was to ensure that my bag, mobile and specs were intact. In the busy Mount Road at 6:30 PM, no one bothered about me. Perhaps they thought I was a drunkard. I got up slowly and quickly checked to see if there was any blood, but found that I had bruises and that was all. Suddenly, I felt old, frustrated, angry, disappointed and helpless. I limped ahead and found a few steps leading to a shop which was closed. There was a dog in one corner. I did not bother and climbed the few steps and then inspected myself. Slowly the bad frustration and helplessness crept up again and I started crying. Maybe I cried for about ten minutes and no one bothered. After all, it was my personal problem. I remembered the famous adage: "when you laugh, the world laughs with you and when you cry, you cry alone." The dog was contemplating going to a better location, and when he saw me crying, he decided that I was harmless and settled down in a better position to relax.

    I got up with a heavy heart, confused mind, a bruised leg and negative thoughts around me. I started walking. I don't know what I was doing – after two hours and ten minutes, I realized that I had walked all the way to Koyambedu. Tired, confused and angry, I got into the first bus, removed my shoes and in no time went to sleep. I was oblivious of what was happening around me, where the bus stopped, who my neighbor was, and whether my bag was safe. I floated and all the memories of the day drifted through me – the nice coffee which my wife gave, the bus journey, the nice lady who traveled with me, the official meeting, the fall and…….. Suddenly, I was shaken up. Somewhere in the distance, I heard the old lady of the morning saying "Bangalore." I thought it was in my dream and I heard myself saying,

"It is okay. We are all going to Bangalore! Relax!" Again, she shook me and I opened my eyes. To my surprise I saw her again and she told me that Bangalore had arrived. Yes! We were at Majestic (Central Bus Station in Bangalore), already. She patted me on my cheek and said, "Young man, relax!"

Suddenly I felt young again. I collected my things and got off. I looked around to thank her. She was nowhere to be seen. I wanted to ask her what her story was for the day. I had mine and every bit of that experience remained with me, alone. I am sure that everyone in this world has stories which make their lives what they are. It is a personal experience that can only be experienced. If narrated to others, it is just communication, just like this one. It means nothing to anyone except for the person himself. Cherish your story and reflect on it. It is yours. It makes your life all the more memorable. This is my story. What is yours?

Motivation – The Process of Transferring Energy

There is a process which is vital for everything in life, but is least understood: Motivation. We all know that Motivation is the energy that keeps people going. The strength of this motivation determines the speed of the achievement of a person. In all related matters, there is no substitute and equivalent to self-motivation. I have always believed that we should not put to inaction our competence just because there is no outside Motivation involved, such as "What will I get?"

Philosophically, I also believe that there is no such thing as external motivation. It is purely short-term negotiation. I have seen several schemes operating in organizations to motivate people. If you achieve a particular result, they will give you additional money or an equivalent. It looks good. Sometimes, it works. I have always wondered whether the opposite is also true. If we remove this "additional money" or incentive, will the person involved not achieve the result? I have some examples which I don't personally believe in, although I am not an authority in this subject. There are instances where people have stopped putting efforts when there is no incentive. I think this is nonsense. If a person CAN, he will do it. If he CANNOT, he will negotiate.

Look at this in another way. Every human being has certain personal goals or objectives for which he is ready to dedicate himself. In the same way, every organization has goals or objectives to which they are willing to commit their resources. As long as there is alignment between these two, the individual's and the organization's objectives, we have no issues. Motivation is not needed. Whatever the individual wants to achieve is the same as what the organization needs. The individual is already motivated. This is the best example of self-motivation. We can also say that there is a natural process in place. On the other hand, if the two objectives don't align, we have a problem. When such a situation exists, the management, with poor vision, resorts to negotiation by

Motivation – The Process of Transferring Energy

doling out incentives, thinking that people can be easily converted to do what the organization wants. I wish that it was that simple!

Introspection reveals something which we all ignore. On the one hand, we already have individuals who are naturally motivated to achieve their goals. We are not willing to recognize this. But, on the other hand, we create a mess by indirectly dampening existing motivation. There is enough proof that artificial methods of motivation aside of self-motivation will work for a very short time only. The best efforts any organization can put in are in aligning the organizational objectives to go closer to the individuals' goals. After all, there is no organization without people.

There is no great organization without great people. Great people are motivated and can do anything. All we have to do is to align the organization's goals with an individual's goals on a very high plane. There already exists self-motivation in every human. The net result is a very good and powerful synergistic harnessing of this power. If we are able to improve our selection process to identify people with good goals and objectives, there is nothing else we need.

All of us have individual points of contacts with others during the course of our daily work life. If we take a few minutes and use this point of contact to share this alignment, there is actually a transfer of energy taking place. But for this to happen, we should have clarity ourselves and also we should be self-motivated. James C Collins, the author of Good to Great very rightly says, "Build an organization first with shared goals and together they will achieve anything."

Reviews to Transfer Seriousness

Review is a serious Management function. There are several forms of review, but the most sustainable one is self-review. If self-reviews are followed by good communication, we have the best results at optimal efficiency. But we should know the objectives of a review. Some reviews are oriented towards internal communication in which case they have to be formally done. There is no other substitute. But in this communication, I am limiting myself to formal reviews.

A few years ago, I was invited by the CEO of a company to attend an internal management review meeting. During the proceedings, I found that they had initiated several projects and were all in various stages of confusion. No clear direction was visible. After the meeting, I had a chance to meet the CEO and asked him why he was not reviewing the projects. What he told me was very surprising. He said that there was no use of reviews! He said that the team members did not do anything on the project and hence it was a waste of time to review. Later in the day, I had a chance to meet some of the actual team members of the projects initiated and asked them why they were not serious when it came to project implementation. What they told me was even more surprising. They said that there was no review at all and no one was interested.

What irony! This company was functioning at a perfect level of useless equilibrium. What was even more intriguing was the fact that the actual meaning of review was lost on these people. That day, I realized that there was some understanding of reviews needed. Most people think that reviews are mainly intended to know the status of an initiative, and to look at what has gone wrong and what has gone right, and why. Consequently, they look at what the next set of corrective actions and targets are. These things may be important, but it is not necessarily the core purpose of a review. That day, I realized that review has the following three crucial objectives. I call them the "Transfer of Seriousness," as the review process plays on psychology. No one wants to get a feeling that things are being dumped on them or that they are doing something which in their opinion is a waste of time:

1. The person to whom a project or initiative is handed over should get the feeling that he has earned this responsibility because of his capability and not because there is no one to take it up or that work was handed over because he had less work.

2. The project or initiative is very important to the company and fits into the overall organizational objective, or that it is essential at that point of time to achieve a major breakthrough – either for problem-solving or improvement.

3. There must be a perception of fairness. People should not get the feeling that they are doing all the work and that others are not involved or that there is no contribution from others. This also refers to the senior management people.

A good review seeks to build the above in the mind of the project leader, so that he feels important and respected. When this is achieved, the leader will do everything to ensure that the work is done. He will get into self-review mode. Instead of spending time on the review of status, we should spend time on transferring this seriousness which can be only the contribution of the top management instead of getting into routine work. It is amazing to see how we can achieve what is right, without talking about it, but by concentrating on the environment around the people. Good culture is not bought, it is built!

A Key Characteristic of the Visionary

This is one subject about which there is no dearth of content to share: competition versus competitiveness. Ever since one is born, there is the start of the trace of competition, only to increase as we grow. Fortunately, this competition, if taken in the right spirit, and if it is fair, teaches us to survive. Having said this, we should not labor under the wrong notion that our ability to survive will start automatically. We have to build it. This counter-ability to fight competition is called competitiveness. Competition is a situation and is external to us. We have no control over it. Competitiveness is a capability and is internal to us. Thus, we have control over it and consequently we have to develop it.

We will discuss this in the context of business only, though it can be extended to anything you are affected by. We can define the rate of competition as the rate at which our business is affected, say the rate at which the market share is eroded, the profitability is eroded, the opportunities are reduced and such else. Similarly, we can define the rate of competitiveness as the rate at which we face the situation, the rate at which we build new capability, we explore new offerings, we explore synergy, we innovate and such else. It is obvious that the rate of competitiveness should be equal to or greater than the rate of competition. But, to be a market leader, the rate of competitiveness should be a few orders of a magnitude higher than the rate of the competition. This kind of order of magnitude advantage cannot be achieved unless we anticipate the need for change, and change rapidly. The following requirements have to be fulfilled:

1. Anticipate the need for change
2. Develop the willingness to change
3. Develop the ability to change

4. Actually, making the change
5. Sustaining the change

A true visionary is needed here. A true visionary is one who not only sees what is coming, but sees it much before anyone else does. Time is the key differentiator. But, it is not as simple as it looks. If someone sees it in advance, that person is dealing with people who are in a different era. Thus, the challenge is much more than one can imagine in each of the above five factors. The depth and power of conviction of the visionary will only determine how it is put across to people. We have always heard of the resistance to change as being a stumbling block. Resistance to change is relative and dependant on time. To overcome resistance to change, one has to use time in an innovative way and make resistance irrelevant. Here starts the key development focus for any management. Take this as a challenge and use your thinking to come up with practical solutions which will make you a better manager and a visionary in the making.

The Inside Story of the Brackets

....

There is another communication in this book on brackets and how brackets can be used for controlling entropy and creating wealth. It was also discussed how brackets can be understood from a Management perspective. I continue with the same concept here and look at another Management dimension which is vital to elevate the spirit of an organization. We learnt that when we are looking at Managing change or when we are going through a crisis like a customer complaint, a not-too-good market scenario or when key people leave and the like, it is essential to apply brackets and use a lot of wisdom to remove the brackets so that the organization does not succumb to deathly pressures.

In this communication, I focus on the principle followed in Algebra to remove brackets. This principle is also a key to sustain organizational value. We know that in Algebra, when we have too many brackets, we start removing the brackets that are inside first and then gradually move outwards till we remove the last bracket. If this principle is not followed, the resultant value is totally different from the truth.

What is the significance from a Management point of view, in removing the brackets which are deep inside first and then start to move outwards? Let us look at the most common reaction of people in any organization to crisis. When there is a customer complaint, most organizations see if this is a complaint meant for us or if it has been sent to us by mistake. Then, they focus on finding external reasons for the complaint, starting with the customer himself, or external forces, generally where we don't have control, such as raw material prices, late incoming material, too much work pressure or a situation where the client has not paid, so he has no right to complain and such else. We start looking at brackets at the outer side, first.

The Inside Story of the Brackets

When a lot of people leave an organization, the tendency is to blame the work environment. The advent of call centers and back office has induced good professionals to go there instead of joining manufacturing. Again, the focus is on looking at brackets which are outside. When profits fall, there is a tendency to blame the political situation, global economic happenings or poor support from bankers and such else. Again, the focus is on brackets which are outside.

Algebra teaches us to look at the innermost brackets first. When we look at this concept for any organization, this is the sickness that is at the center in an organization and is deep-rooted and generally classified as chronic issues. Chronic issues come from our own thinking, attitudes, complacence, glory of past successes and the ego offshoot, the lack of discipline, the lack of internal communication, the lack of team work and so on. These things will never go away even if we look at the brackets close to the outside.

On the other hand, brackets that are outside, work like protection. With them on guard, we can look internally and address the issues that can be solved only by us. One example of having such an external protection is to reduce the order load and start working internally. Cleaning the inner mess is a top priority. When the inner mess is addressed and removed gradually, inner strength starts to grow. When inner strength starts growing, it is easier to remove other brackets. When the last bracket is removed, we have no fear or tension or anxiety.

This principle has a close parallel to Problem-Solving, but at a higher level. For instance, recognizing that there is a problem is the first step in problem-solving. A part of this ability to see problems comes from our ability and confidence in solving problems. If we can solve problems, we can see problems. Otherwise, the problem is ignored as there is no solution anyway. Brackets help us look at problems as they will allow us to separate different issues and improve our abilities to see properly. Once the problem is seen, we have to apply brackets sufficiently as they contain and isolate and do not allow it to spread further. Once the problem is contained, with the brackets in place, we can change our mindset to clean the internal reasons first and then the external reasons. When this cleaning is done, we remove the brackets allowing us to grow even better, thus making the famous saying come

■ I Will Make It Happen

true – problems are the starting point for improvement. We start with a problem, apply brackets, clean the internal mess and remove the brackets, and then present a new picture of the organization and then, leap into the future.

Nested brackets

$$2(x - [3 - 2(y - 5x)])$$
$$= 2(x - [3 - 2y + 10x])$$
$$= 2(x - 3 + 2y - 10x)$$
$$= 2x - 6 + 4y \ldots$$

Predict the Prediction and Lead the Control

I cannot resist getting back into a few basics in statistics, again. Hopefully these tiny bits of interpretation can get all of you interested in learning statistics. I guess this is a huge service we can do to the world of business. The subject is prediction and predictability. The word statistical refers to this important principle of predictability in life and business. The sustenance and success of a business is dependent on the underlying predictability, be it process or effort and the result or output.

Profit should be predictable. Planning should be predictable in terms of delivery. Expenses should be predictable. Human performance should be predictable. Attitude should be predictable. Absenteeism should be predictable. The list is endless. In fact, the Six Sigma philosophy (a statistics based Systematic problem-solving process) encourages us to establish the right measures, develop a process for its achievement, understand the full process to ensure that the measures are predictable, and keep gaining knowledge to fine tune your understanding, while bringing all the other related factors like time, money, efficiency, and such else under their respective targets. With this, we have Holistic Enterprise Objectives Delivery and Performance.

What is predictability? Having an expectation and getting the performance or result close to these expectations with minimum variation around it, is a very simple and useful understanding of predictability. There are two types of predictions:

1. Point Prediction
2. Interval Prediction

Point prediction refers to a very important, essential and highly expected but almost impossible expectation. It refers to the expectation such as what exact time you will come to the office the next day, or what the exact profit we will achieve next month be like, or what the exact absenteeism will be the next day, and so on. You will immediately see that this is true knowledge, but unfortunately, there is no scientific way to get an answer.

Interval prediction, on the other hand, is very practical but difficult to understand concept and perhaps use at any point of time. Interval prediction refers to the expectation –such as within what time interval you will arrive, within what limits our profit will lie in the coming month, within what percentage limits our absenteeism will fall tomorrow and such else. To get an answer to this question is very easy using statistical theories. This is exactly what we mean when we refer to prediction in statistical terminology. Once you understand the concept of prediction, and accept that we have enough knowledge to estimate Interval Prediction, you already have the answer to a Management culture which Dr. Deming refers to as the Culture of Statistical Thinking. Here is how we do it.

Once you have an interval prediction, we can direct all our resources to learn and plan so that we continuously reduce this interval to smaller limits till we actually reach an equivalent of Point Prediction. Our wisdom grows to such an extent that we have the real knowledge to reach a situation which God alone can achieve. Anyone who appreciates this theory will easily see what the control chart is doing and the direction of improvement, which is stemming from the chart. The same is the underlying understanding in Measurement System Analysis. In the Control Chart, there is no better way to understand and interpret the Attribute Control Charts such as np, p, c and u charts (these are Control charts for Attribute Data. For more information read any book on SPC) – especially when our expectation is to get ZERO defects, people cannot easily understand what the control limits signify.

Predictability is same as Control. But improvement is different from control. Both are important objectives for any organization. To have a sustained and systematic program of improvement, we should have control, first. Control allows us to plan. Improvements can be planned properly when there is predictability. We should not achieve improvement by accident. Improvement should be strategic, well thought out, well executed, well achieved and well controlled. Control comes before and after improvement. This concept is well written by Dr. Juran (An eminent Quality Teacher) in his classical book, Quality Control Handbook. I recommend reading this. Let us start the journey of achieving spectacular results by first entering the world of control!

The First Half Is the Other Half of the Second Half

As humans, we cannot resist the question: "Who is better?" We always want to prove that we are better and try to find means to prove this point, so much so that we miss the essence of living. This is true in married lives where many couples use the first years of their marriage to justify that they are better and keep finding endless faults in the other. There is no reason to doubt the statement - "If you look, you will find it!"

We can extend this logic in organizations where teams spend more time in finding who is better or employees within the same department try to prove that they are better, so much so that instead of working together, they start competing with each other. Now comes the question, "Who is better?" Is the marketing person who gets the order better or is the person who executes it better? Is the person who gives the address better or is the person who locates the destination using the address better? Is the person who teaches better or is the student who grasps and learns better? Is the manager running a department better or are the people working with the manager better? Is an experienced person better or is a new trainee better? Interesting questions, with interesting answers.

In a country like India, invariably, hierarchy prevails irrespective of what is right. This is also true with elders, experienced persons, wealthy people and people in position of authority and so on. We have an extraordinary ability to bury our personal desires, feelings, knowledge and ethics and so on, to live in a false world of satiating others in the spirit of keeping the wheels running. On the other hand, indiscriminate approaches based on first impressions, first emotions, mob psychology, immature thought process, etc. are equally dangerous.

What is missing is a very important question. What is the truth? Unfortunately, truth is never known in its entirety, and sometimes never. Perhaps this is the will of God in running the world, which you look at things from your focus and form judgments and actions. Winning or losing is only a matter of perception and stems from personal standards. What goes on always is the learning and understanding which we form of ourselves, people, society and this world.

But let us look at the original question in a different way. Who is better?

Let us look at the dynamics. All this is team work. No one succeeds alone. There is a contribution from everyone. The contribution may look insignificant but is nevertheless very strong. A song you hear in the neighborhood. A smile from an elderly person while walking. A phone call from a wrong number – they had all contributed to keep you away from something else. A chance meeting with someone in the train, An associate who does small portions of your work. A fellow participant who asks a question which makes you learn better are all examples of contributions which have an impact.

What comes out is a very comfortable feeling. It is not about who is better. It is the fact that everyone is essential for results. Instead of comparing, try to understand that they are absolutely needed for your progress. When you embrace this feeling, you will return something to all of your acquaintances, even very trivial things like an apology or gratitude, a smile or a pat which may be insignificant for you, but goes a long way in a very non-linear and extraordinary way for their progress. We need everyone, and everyone needs us. We are some part of the micro structure called life. Without a very tiny bit, the whole structure collapses, leaving us very poor and weak. Learn the important lesson. You are not privileged to be in any part of the wheel. You are privileged to be a part of the wheel.

■ I Will Make It Happen

Controlled Production – The Central Focus in ISO 9001

The QMS – ISO 9001 has a very interesting clause on Controlled Production. What could be the meaning of this requirement? What is Controlled Production? Is it running production under controlled conditions? Or is it controlling the production as per customer needs? Or, is it running production so that there are no abnormal situations? There could be several explanations. Let us look at what makes maximum sense to the Management.

Controlled should mean that something is expected, and the output is according to those expectations. In other words, there is a leaning towards expectations. Expectations automatically mean that we go into the domain of forecast or predictability. Predictability could mean control. In SPC, we say a process is under Statistical Control but that does not mean that the production process is under the control of statisticians. It means that we run a process under a predictable output situation. Let us look at what is expected from a production. A little introspection reveals several things, which we call as the first set of requirements:

- It should be as per the quantity designed or using the installed capacity.
- It should be as per the quality levels capable of being achieved and agreed upon with the customer
- It should be at the levels of cost target which could mean a decent profit for the company and still be competitive

Obviously, all these things would mean a second set of requirements as follows:

- Good efficiency of material conversion – minimum waste

> Machines and equipments not being operated more than the rated capacity
> Producing with the skill levels available
> Maintaining optimum inventory levels
> Ensuring that factory space is well utilized
> Ensuring that there is no Unnecessary movement of material

Experts will argue that there is no meaning in achieving the first by sacrificing the second set of requirements. But, the strength of our convictions should be such that there is no way we can achieve the first set without adhering to the second set. Logically, we should design a system which will automatically give the first set of requirements when the second set is complied with. Let us take this forward and try to imagine what ISO 9001 would have as its intent.

The biggest enemies of Controlled Production are inspection and verification. If we have to resort to checking as a means to have Controlled Production, we are already building waste into the system. Therefore, we have to imagine a way of working where we follow a step-by-step approach and we get a repeatable, predictable and expected production output. This output comes not by inspection and correction, but by following actions based on real-time situations. This step-by-step approach is not something we can buy from the market or get from a customer. It is something we have to develop and establish, document and then train people to follow.

This involves study and repeated study. Obviously, we are not expected to have this when we demonstrate the system for certification. The certification process only evaluates whether we have this understanding. We are capable of defining internal process measures, which will be like guide posts in ensuring that we reach controlled production. Perhaps here is a clue as to how we should understand non-conforming situations and their associated actions. Non-conforming situations are not events for which we have to go defensive and find a quick way out. Non-conforming situations are pointers that we have not yet reached the controlled state, and hence, we should work continuously on the development of the system which means study and repeated study. Real success lies in the details – small technical aspects which are otherwise treated as insignificant and ignored.

Controlled Production does not come accidentally. It comes from dedicated effort in understanding technology by creating glory around smaller things which are technically very significant. Let us harness the power of learning by first defining something to measure, then tracking it, then creating a system to achieve it. Based on the result, keep adjusting the system till we get the results in a predictable manner, and learn to learn systematically.

The Dynamics of the Circle around Us

Let us get a look at Psychology, now. Have you noticed that we get certain ambiguous reactions at certain times from the same individual? For instance, we consider someone close to us and keep moving with that person in a particular way. Suddenly, one day you notice that you get a different and confusing response, even when your approach has been the same. This is where we have to understand the theory of circles. Every human has a circle around him. If anyone else gets closer and tries to enter that circle, the person becomes very uncomfortable. This circle is so powerful that for some people, when we try to come closer physically, the person backs away. Sometimes, it is in the form of what we say. When you try to discuss certain topics, the person becomes uncomfortable. Thus, the manifestation of this circle is in several forms.

Further, this circle expands and contracts on two counts

1. Different times
2. Different people

The circle shrinks or expands depending on the person who is interacted with, and also in different circumstances. Imagine this circle as a storehouse of energy. This energy is sent and received continuously, like a transmitter and receiver. Sometimes, the energy meets its favorable counterpart. That is why we find close relationships existing between certain people.

It is easy to decipher that the wider the circle, the more is the influential zone of that person. Widening the circle is the ability of the individual, but many things are inherent. One should also be careful as there are false indicators of the width. Take the following example. Depending on the position or responsibility played by the person, there is a functional requirement to show a different circle. For instance, the marketing or public relations or the HR person has many times to put a different circle in the interest of the function that is being handled. But, when the person is in private, the circle shrinks back to its true size. This is the first reason why we get ambiguous reactions from people when we judge the person to be having a different circle.

The second reason why conflicting reactions occur is emotion. Sometimes, when there is success, the person suddenly depicts a bigger circle which is valid only for a short period of time. Likewise, the circle shrinks when there is a negative emotion. Now, imagine what will happen when several combinations of circle size and strength of the energy radiated interact with different individuals who depict their own pattern of energy. It will be an interesting statistical model which can predict the cumulative density of this situation. Hence, there is no need to worry about ambiguous reactions as long as we understand that we also do the same thing to others. Never be judgmental. Try to understand the context and develop a communication pattern which has a density that can give you a minimum success during interactions. Maturity comes when we know how to play the interaction pattern depending on the situation and invariably, the first few seconds are enough to judge where the circle is.

But, we should never forget that there is a certain minimum circle size which is inherited by any person. That is the true character. This true character can change dramatically only on one condition, when it is destroyed and regrouped, when a person gets a serious jolt in life: like when some events have a deep impact on a person, like a rebirth, or like a certain awakening when the conscious level changes totally. When management considers change in any organization, it is of paramount importance to understand this and create an approach and structure that is capable of destroying and recreating a different and favorable circle. Asking if this is possible is asking a wrong question. How one should make this possible, is the right question and the only learning which the Management should attempt. Any takers for this?

■ I Will Make It Happen

Can Internal Auditing Be the Most Welcome Process in a Company?

Let us spend some time on the core strength of the certified system, like ISO 9001: the Auditing System. Let us look at Auditing a System. It is perhaps a very interesting question to see if there is anyone who likes auditing. There are three parties involved: the auditor, the auditee and the people linked to the system that is being audited, apart from the function directly audited. Let us restrict ourselves to the internal auditing, where the objectives are not just demonstrating compliance, but a deeper motive of sustaining the system and leading it to the next generation.

Let us look at the following situation. On a particular day – say January 1 – a company gets certified to a system like QMS ISO 9001. What does this certification mean internally? It does not mean that they have a wonderful system. It does not mean that there are no issues anywhere. It does not mean that the system is working well. It just means that at that particular time, the collective maturity of the people working in the system matches some average predicted output of a documented system. The real enablers of the performance are not what the standard says, but what the internal process is that which enables the company to function and meet its goals.

Let us imagine what happens six months later, say on June 1. It is quite possible that some people have attended training programs on varied matters, and that their maturity and competence has grown. Some people just become wise by repeatedly practicing something. Some people become better equipped when they deal with different customers and different requirements. Some people learn better ways of doing things by watching others or adopting the latest and most appropriate technology. The net result of all these is that the organization has moved several steps up. Here, 'UP' means anything better than before, which means, moving towards improvement. But the documented system remains at the same level, at least in most cases, except where there is already internal wisdom which keeps pace with people's maturity. There is a definite gap between how people now think, act, behave and what is documented.

Now comes internal auditing and the auditor. It is almost certain that the auditor will detect this gap and this will be reported as an observation. Depending on the maturity of the auditor, it could be classified as non-conformity. Now, comes the dilemma. The auditee and those related would feel that they are better than the system, while the auditor will feel that they have strayed from the system.

The auditor has a great responsibility in deciphering whether this gap is not just a random variation, but a definite shift. In statistical language, we call it a statistically significant shift. The auditor can get into "misses" or "false alarms" while taking this decision. More important is the psychology of the auditee who feels that he is dragged down from his elevated position which has come from genuine competence enhancement. The internal auditing system will cry for compliance, and the net result is poorly accepted compliance, a deep-rooted hate for the system and a tit-for-tat approach across the organizational interface.

That is why the QMS Standard ISO 9001 clearly mentions that the Management responsible for the area should take timely action. The corrective action is no longer a business between the auditor and auditee or the Management Representative. The entire Management team should look at this issue and direct system corrections – if there is genuine people growth, to once again match the system to the collective maturity of the organization. If this is not done, then the system will remain a vegetable to be dragged along with the functioning of the organization with resentment everywhere.

When the system is corrected to reflect the current maturity, it is welcomed by everyone, and people look forward to the next audit. It is a very natural extension to understand and look for evidence of changes in the system processes when targets for the various measures are changed each year. It is impossible to achieve differing targets with the same documented system. Has the Management understood this correctly? Look at the spirit of this glorious standard. Long live the QMS Standard!

My Dear SPC – Please Walk By My Side

I am restricting myself only to SPC (Statistical Process Control) here. There are many misconceptions about SPC - for instance that it is applicable only for the manufacturing industry, it is applicable only when mass production exists or that there are a lot of statistics involved and such else. All of these are not true as the fundamental principle behind SPC is so unique and the application is so much open to imagination that I thought of sharing a few points here.

What is the difference between Process Control and Statistical Process Control? Process Control can be viewed as having three distinct phases:

1. Observation or Measurement
2. Judgment
3. Taking Action

Example – driving a scooter or the heat treatment process. Take driving the scooter, for instance. What is process control as per the above three points? While driving, we observe the speed and where we are. We know when we have to reach and where. Then, we make a judgment on whether we will be able to achieve this objective at the current speed or not. Based on our judgment, we either accelerate or continue on the same speed and keep doing this continuously till we reach our destination. This is process control. If this is understood well, why do we need SPC? We can continue with process control and be happy. Don't ever think that we do SPC for the collection of data and to study historic data and analyzing it. There must be a deeper meaning for having the S in SPC which is very different from process control and can give us better results.

Why do we need the Statistics in Process Control? How do we understand SPC holistically?

SPC should be viewed as:

S – Stability

P – Performance

C – Control

Incidentally, this is the order in which the SPC development has to take place. Any process has to be first studied for its stability. This also means predictability. Even if a process does not produce non-conforming parts, there is no guarantee that it will continue to do the same unless there is predictability. Predictability can be checked by using a histogram giving a normal or bell-shaped pattern. The science of statistics gives several methods to test predictability.

If the process is not predictable, there is no meaning in doing any analysis as there is no guarantee that it will repeat. Further we have to keep doing this analysis every time we produce. This is why we see many companies have so much faith in 100% inspection as they are not sure of predictability. There are even examples of companies practicing SPC but still doing 100 % inspection.

The process of studying stability allows us to understand the causes which affect predictability. This knowledge is needed for us to control the same process later. The causes affecting predictability are referred to as Assignable Causes. They can be understood as time-related causes. For example, take clamping in drilling. We should know when to adjust the clamping based on the quantity of production and not quality of the part. This is called time-based control. Once stability is established, we look at performance. Here, performance means the ability to meet the Product Quality Requirement.

In SPC literature, this is referred as Pp, Cp, Ppk and Cpk (These are process capability indices. Refer any book on SPC). The total variation in the process should be less than the tolerance. For a Cp of 1.33, the total variation should be 75% of the tolerance. This only means that you have a cushion to run the process with fewer restrictions on the control of the process parameters under the hope that you can reduce cost and be more competitive. This has to be exploited commercially. Otherwise, no company will respect us and the SPC.

■ I Will Make It Happen

Finally, we have control. Control of process is not controlling the quality of the product. It only refers to the management of Assignable Causes. If we know when we have to adjust the process so that the effect of the time-related assignable cause does not distort predictability, we can speed up the process till that time. Then adjust and then speed up and so on. After all, the objective of any company should be to produce the desired quality at the fastest rate, and with the lowest cost. Many of us believe that this is not possible and argue that if we want quality, delivery will be affected or cost will be more. This logic is fundamentally faulty as no management wants this. We have to demonstrate that SPC can give this quality with the lowest cost and the fastest delivery. Let us master this art of understanding and the management of process and restore faith in SPC across all applications.

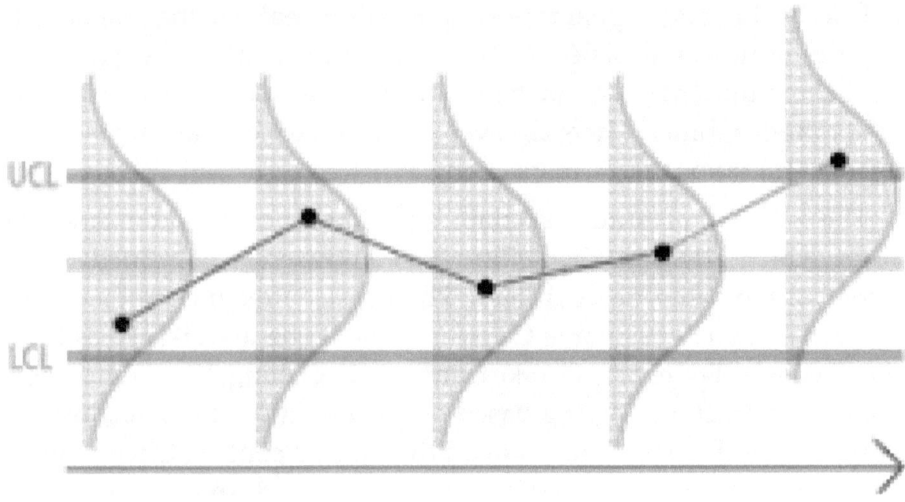

A System Shall Be Defined, Documented, Implemented, Maintained and Improved

The ISO 9001 QMS states under System documentation, "A system shall be defined, documented, implemented, maintained and improved." This is not difficult to understand. But let me lead you all through a deeper understanding as follows:

DEFINED: When the ISO 9001 standard was first published, there were so many loose statements like ISO 9001 is very simple, or that all you have to do is to document what you do and do what you document. This is a very wrong understanding. If you document what you do and do what you document, you will get what you have always got. If you wish to get benefits from the system, we should first review what we are doing in line with our objectives and then do all that is needed to achieve the objectives and then document it. This is the right understanding. Take for example a company which wishes to improve its business by 20% as an objective, the following things are to be done before documenting:

1. Ensure that this objective is understood by all.
2. Identify those functions in the company which impact this objective like Marketing, Engineering, Production, Human Resource, etc.
3. In each of these functions, review and identify what processes are to be developed or modified. Some examples are: Marketing, new enquiry generation, engineering, new product development, production, capacity utilization or enhancement, HR, Manpower build-up.
4. Check whether these processes already exist. If they exist, review whether they are adequate to achieve the 20% growth.

If not, identify what needs to be done extra to achieve the objectives of 20% growth. If the process does not already exist, identify those processes in line with the process approach.
5. Get the agreement with everyone concerned and then we are ready with the DEFINE part.

DOCUMENTED: Documenting is not paperwork, though it is one of the expressions of documentation. The real meaning of documentation is communication. Hence, the format, style and language are not important, as it has to be done in such a way that the document matches the culture and maturity of the organization. It should be effective in the sense that people are clear about what is expected of them and when they should execute actions and when they should escalate. Documentation can be visual control as well, as it has an immediate impact. What is documented should be so well written that anyone can follow it and do their work. In a way, a good documentation is also de-skilling. Hence, it is a very economic outcome for the company

IMPLEMENTED: This is the starting point of validation. Unless you implement, we don't know whether it is possible to practice. There is no point sitting on the wall and imagining whether the documented system can be implemented or not. Obviously, we should face problems initially, as people struggle to stretch themselves to practice. Based on the response from a statistically significant sample, we should undertake immediate corrections to the documented system. In other areas, we should give sufficient time for mental changes to take place and people getting used to compliance. A key aspect of learning in implementation is the interface between various functions: management, communication, feedback, integration and such else. We have to ensure that proper triggers are there in each process to enable the applicable interface process to act when necessary. For example, when a new person joins, the training process should be activated. When a new machine arrives, the process capability evaluation should be activated.

MAINTAINED: The difference between implemented and maintained is the angle of continuity. Implementation can be considered as a one-time action, whereas maintenance is continued implementation. This is the starting point of cultural change. Also, impractical aspects of a system will come when we start practicing continuously. Such aspects should be promptly addressed for getting a suitable and effective system.

Internal Audits play a very important role in maintenance. Maintenance is not routine compliance though compliance is an index to be studied. Imagine the following situation. When you start the implementation of a system, the system contents match with the maturity and knowledge of the people in the company. As time passes, people are trained and know newer things and their maturity and knowledge improves and becomes better, whereas the system remains at that level. Internal audits have to understand this gap and then modify the system to match the new maturity of the people. It should not go the other way of making people leave what they have learnt and start practicing the same things which were documented earlier.

IMPROVED: This is the continuous improvement angle. This means setting new targets for the objectives or setting new objectives and the whole process starts all over again. One aspect of improvement is capability building. So, the system should drive this important function of capability enhancement. When new targets are set or new objectives are set, the process has to change from a capability angle. The same process will not be suitable. One example is the speed of performance. Can the system improve the speed of the organization? Can the system eliminate waste so that better productivity levels are achieved? Another aspect is the technology of documentation – paperless, electronic medium, automation, etc. – which are all the requirements of the next generation.

The best way to address this is by looking external and at all stakeholders – customers, suppliers, employees, and the future generation – and start to think from their perspective. Last but not the least, input is the PDCA cycle of learning from all corrective and preventive actions undertaken and filtering the knowledge gained into the documented system. Embrace the system and show the path to the world that this simple system can achieve whatever objectives we set out to achieve.\

■ I Will Make It Happen

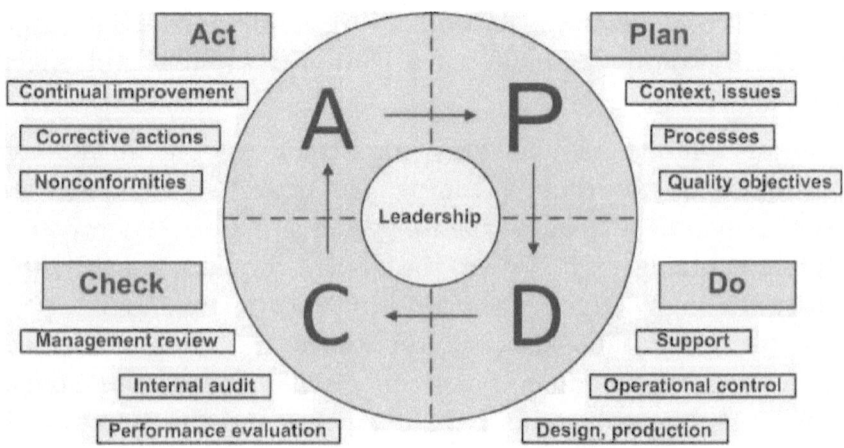

The Inherent Music in Variation

Vibration and Variation. Sound is a form of vibration. Depending on the frequency and amplitude, we have different forms like infrasonic, sonic and ultrasonic. Our ears are used to the sonic range only. However, in engineering we have several applications of the usage of ultrasonic sound and there are cases where infrasonic sound has brought down buildings. These are just a few illustrations to demonstrate the power of vibrations. There are also mystic examples of vibrations connecting people from different physical locations.

Variation is a truth with which we all have to learn to cope with. Variation is inherent in nature and depending on how well we understand variation and its causes; we can manage processes to deliver results as per the next processe's expectations. It makes tremendous economic sense to master the understanding of variation, which ultimately leads us to knowledge which can be used for the control of the very same variation with which we started. Having understood the basics, let us look at a little analogy between sound and quality through vibration and variation.

While silence is golden, sound is required, music is pleasing - noise is a problem. Sometimes, silence is nice, but many times, it is very scary and we all prefer some sound. If sound can be controlled to give a pleasing experience to the ears, we have music and overdoing this without control is noise. Similarly, in the output of processes, there is the concept of variation. Let us start with no or zero variation. If there is no variation, it looks like a perfect process. But alike silence, it is scary as we have no way to compare anything. Just like the necessity of sound, some variation is also needed. This variation gives us the experience of life and the starting point of learning. We always learn by comparison. A child hears a word and when he hears it again, he compares and learns. We learn a concept and when we hear a similar concept, we compare and learn. Likewise, a process variation is a must to compare and learn. This variation should be controlled, like music is. This is what we call as the inherent variation in the process. If this inherent variation is stable, akin to normal distribution, then we have a peaceful management process. This is similar to enjoying music.

If everything is predictable, then there is no more learning. Hence, we have to experiment now and then to look for better things. This is the principle of continuous improvement. When we do experiments with music, we disturb the rhythm and get different vibrations. Sometimes, it is unbearable and gets into the domain of noise. Likewise, when we experiment with processes we are sometimes faced with excessive variation and this is very disturbing. It is important to learn that great wizards of music play with vibrations and give us even better pleasing sound and some even greater wizards control the excessive vibration and give us a new form of music. Likewise, process experimenters should not be wary of variation and boldly experiment and arrive at better stable processes or master the variations to such an extent that they can generate what they want, when they want and how they want. Masters are not born but are created by their own ability to see through and distill the causal mechanism so much that they effortlessly do and undo what they want.

God. Are you listening? Are you one of us or are we one of you?

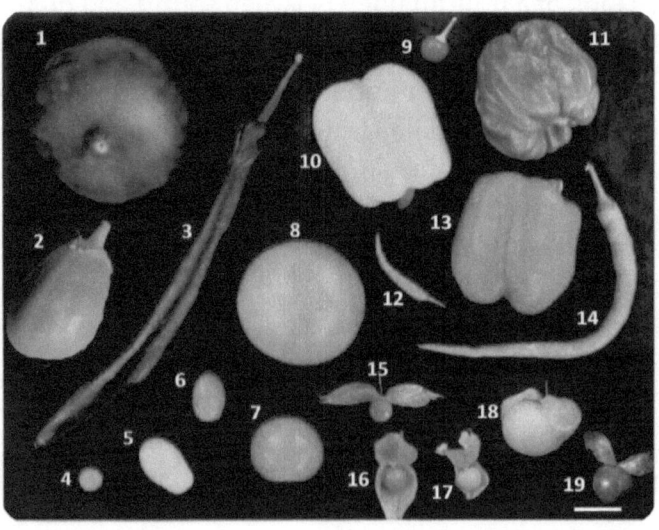

Shared Vision – The Collective Power of an Organization

This is another great idea from the stables of Physics into the house of Management. There is infinite power in synergy. It is well known that when the frequency in an induced state matches the natural frequency of a system, the amplitude multiplies uncontrollably to destruction. That is why, when soldiers march on a bridge, they are always asked to break the rhythm of their march so that there is no chance of the frequency to match with the natural frequency of the bridge and thus, the bridge and the soldiers are saved.

Now, we turn to management. If there is synergy between thought and action, between plan and execution, between intention and display, then there is a realization of wealth. Most of us are concerned with all of these as an integral part of our existence. But, simple things should not be ignored or taken for granted. Let us look at this analogy. It is said that the aircraft follows the direction of the nose when in air and the direction of the wheel when on ground. This could be a very insignificant or matter-of-fact information from a knowledge point of view. But, it is a very significant and genuinely true from a Management point of view. The analogy of air and ground in an aircraft is similar to planning and execution, thoughts and action, intention and display from any organizational stand point.

It is very important that there is an alignment between the nose and wheel as far as reaching the destination is concerned. But, in an organizational context, there is no necessity to have any physical alignment. As long as there is a strategic alignment with a full organization level cooperation then we have the same delivery like the aircraft. Strategic alignment is not easy to achieve. Here, the word strategy has to be understood as a "Direction Inducing Action." This is very important while planning and execution. There is one way to achieve this as a natural process and that is by having "Shared Vision." There are so many situations in our management life where we have to think and take decisions. There are so many people who will be doing this. There is no way in which we can teach any uniform rule or procedure to do this. But still, there should be strategic alignment. No one can imagine what situation will arise and what decision is right or what action is right. But, if there is a common vision and that is shared by everyone concerned, the overall direction is protected. Under that circumstance, all thoughts, decisions and actions will fall in place towards the direction dictated by the vision. This is called strategic alignment.

Otherwise, we will have a very good plan by a set of people who are like being in the air and follow their nose. We have another set of people who are firm on ground and they act very well in the direction of the wheel. But, there is no guarantee that there is an alignment between these two and we only end up getting a resultant achievement. This resultant achievement is sometimes even less than the sum of the parts - let alone getting synergistic and exponential results. Shared vision is a least understood phenomenon simply because it is taken for granted in a semantic format. Let us not underestimate the power of shared visions and ensure that the aircraft-like organization generates its designed wealth through its inbuilt capability, i.e., the collective power of its people.

The Art of Looking – The Intelligent Camera

Innocence is not knowing, Inefficiency is not seeing, Foolishness is not recognizing and Ineffectiveness is not acting. We all end up somewhere in this cycle. No one is perfect. We all get into any of the above at different times. While this is not a point to be worried about, not learning is the greatest ill. In this essay, we are not restricting ourselves to the simple form of using eyes to see. Here, we bring forward the traditional seeing, backed by the intent of the mind and the life-giving quality of the heart. There are three forms of looking:

1. Looking at the same level and around 360 degrees
2. Looking down
3. Looking up

Most of us are so blinded with arrogance that we don't see when we should see. We feel that we are above all the people or things which we see at our level, so much so, that we miss the variety and smartness of our fellow beings and things. When we look down, we generally look down with contempt and convey the message that we are above all so much so that we don't realize that what we see down are pointers to what is eventually going to come: the future. Lastly, when we look up, we only look up when we are in distress and seek the divine support for whatever we wish to accomplish.

What a waste of the divine faculties bestowed on us by God! Let us apply this principle for one common and useful concept: training. Let us start with "looking up." No support can ever be provided if we are not ready to receive it. Looking up is a waste when we have not internally provided openings for whatever we want to reach us. Take a training program. Before attending any session, prepare yourself and be clear as to what you don't know and provide the mental openings for receiving the knowledge. Otherwise, the best of the faculty will end

■ I Will Make It Happen

up as a one-way communicator. So, looking up to a training session is to be backed by a set of systematic preparatory actions.

Likewise, when you are conducting a program, it is a very easy virtue to "look down" on the participants. "Oh. They don't know even fundamentals." Instead, concentrate on your learning first, to find the easiest way to transfer knowledge and to find openings which do not offer resistance, rather than bringing up resistance as an excuse for the lack of effectiveness. Finally, there is no better way to improve effectiveness in life than to park and share knowledge among colleagues, i.e., "looking around." Many of us have a tendency to look at our colleagues as competitors and hence, there is a total lack of will to share anything. The theory of constraints teaches us that the strength of the whole system is in the weakest link. Just upgrading yourself is no use unless there is a collective effort to strengthen the weak link. Don't just look around, up or down. Look with meaning and contribute to the overall flow. There is no value in stagnation. Value is generated when there is flow. We will look at flow and energy as a continuation to this concept in another chapter.

The Art of Receiving and Giving

In this communication, we see a very important extension to seeing that of receiving and giving, just like seeing, receiving and giving are also pertinent dimensions in our useful work life. Nature and certain lessons from physics are relevant forever. We will explore one such combination today around the subject of energy.

When you look up and when you are ready, you start receiving knowledge, learning, energy or life itself. Physics teaches us that when something comes down from a higher level, there is a conversion of potential energy to kinetic energy. The kinetic energy is with velocity and force. Hence, we must be prepared to receive this. Whether you are attending a training program or you are receiving knowledge from the position of a good student, you have to be careful not to be swept away by the emotion of what and how certain things are taught. A good student is like a dam which ensures that there is no breakage, no washing away and no waste. What should really be washed away are unnecessary emotions, negative energy and resistance to change.

All energy that is received has a place and should be safe. When the velocity is reduced, there is certain calmness. This period of calmness is the time to temper emotions and ensure smooth distribution into all possible space. One must learn with passion and the force of knowledge should be distributed during the days following the learning experience to position it all around us, in the systems, culture and the very atmosphere of the organization, and above all, in our very being. Allow reflection and follow up actions to calm the various forces and allow the beauty of what we have learnt to surface and manifest itself in a ready-to-apply condition, in all apertures, positions, structure of the organization. Just like a dam ensures that there is conservation of mass and energy, this calming is a must for knowing the effectiveness of what we have learnt.

Unconsciously, we are now building potential energy back from the kinetic energy. Now, the energy is ready to be delivered to the next level.

Now, we have the chance to reconvert the potential energy into kinetic energy when we teach others. Don't be in too much excitement to deliver all that you know of. Use the learning you had when you received the kinetic energy and gently unleash the power to the next level, and enable them to receive energy with the right force. If this is done properly, there is no waste in the next chain of learning. Now, it is up to the next level to convert kinetic energy into another potential energy for further dissipation.

The law of nature will ensure that there is some loss unless we add or sort of top up at each level. This is the subject of adaptation. A good adaptation will ensure that the energy is loaded into smaller streams or vehicles where there is further focus and forcefulness. Adaptation is the process of maintaining the spirit of the subject but modifying the delivery vehicle to suit the receiver's stature and embedding in a smaller vehicle which navigates the energy to touch the right spot of the receiver. This right spot should trigger an irreversible, positive, self-sustaining and explosive opening up which creates better and value-based opportunities.

This is like taking a picture in the camera and then converting it into a usable medium and imprinting it in the right places in the right quantity for others to enjoy and use.

The Art of Receiving and Giving

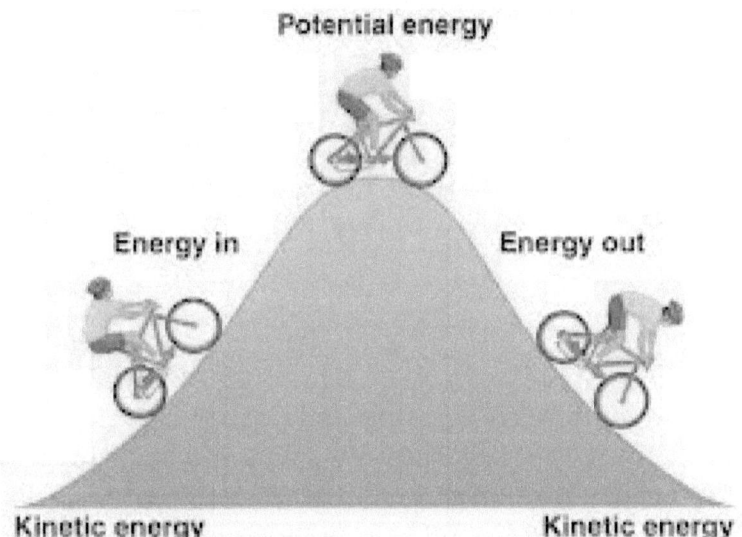

The Story of the Median – The Unsung Hero

....

Let us understand a reality right. There are people and there are contributions. If we had a perfect measure of contribution, which is giving the right weight to tangible and intangible performance, then we have a good system. Unfortunately, in most management systems, the measurement of performance is tilted towards what can be easily measured. A key failure is that people who enable the contribution are rarely recognized, and the ones who can show performance are invariably recognized. Maybe we should, sometimes, have a system which is not only concerned about the actual performance, but also on the relative intrinsic strengths of the number of people who exist in an organization. Let us visit statistics again, but this time, the Median.

The Median, the Mean and the Mode are the "Trimurti" (an Indian word meaning Three Great Personalities) of central tendency. The Median is that value that divides data into two equal parts. The fundamental difference between the Mean and the Median lies in their content and approach. The Mean is concerned about values whereas Median is concerned only with numbers. In a way, both represent values, but the Median gives an added dimension of equality. In Mean, we start with each value whereas in Median, we start by looking at the total number.

In life, both, value and number are important. If there are several readings, mean is that value which is derived by adding all the observations and dividing by the total number of readings. On the other hand, the Median picks up one value which divides the data into two parts. There will be an equal number of items on either side of the Median while there is no necessity that there should be an equal number of readings on either side of the mean. If there are heavy weights, the mean tends towards one side. But Median is not concerned about heavy weights. It is more concerned that we divide all the items into equal parts.

Many times, measure is not always the right indicator. In any organization, every member is important. Just because an executive is strong, we cannot be biased in his favor. A clerk or receptionist are equally important and have very profound contributions to make to the success of the executive or the organization. This is what the Median teaches us. It teaches us to respect everyone and put them on either side, in an equal number, demonstrating that everyone is important and is included. There are several functions in a company like the Top Management, Finance, the HR and Administration. They should not treat people based on their visible contributions alone. There are so many intrinsic contributions that can never be measured. A good HR manager who goes across to everyone in the morning with a pleasant smile or a Quality Manager who teaches everyone about the merits of prevention are the ones that are sought after, these days.

Contributions are important as they help a company survive. But, it is not prudent to think that people who are showing contributions alone are important. There are many people behind the scenes who do as much to enable the so-called contributors to contribute. While Mean offers an indication and leans towards heavy weights, Median always remains firm and keeps everyone in good spirits after putting them in a natural order – either ascending or descending. No one is alone and no performance is unique. Each has its own set of interdependent contributors. Recognizing all of these is a key role of the Management.

What better indicator can be used, than the Median? The Median does not divide performance into two equal parts. But the Median says, if I have ten people, I will divide them equally in some order. It gives a feeling to the people belonging to one segment that there are equal number on the other side.

Future research should come with a measure that mixes people and divides them equally, so that there is a level-playing field in the company. Median is a better motivator as it does not support heavy weights and in an organization, being unbiased is a strong virtue. Never get confused on this. Median is still a value but it is that value which has equal number of people on either side. This is management

■ I Will Make It Happen

strength of being unbiased. Now use your imagination to understand Median better.

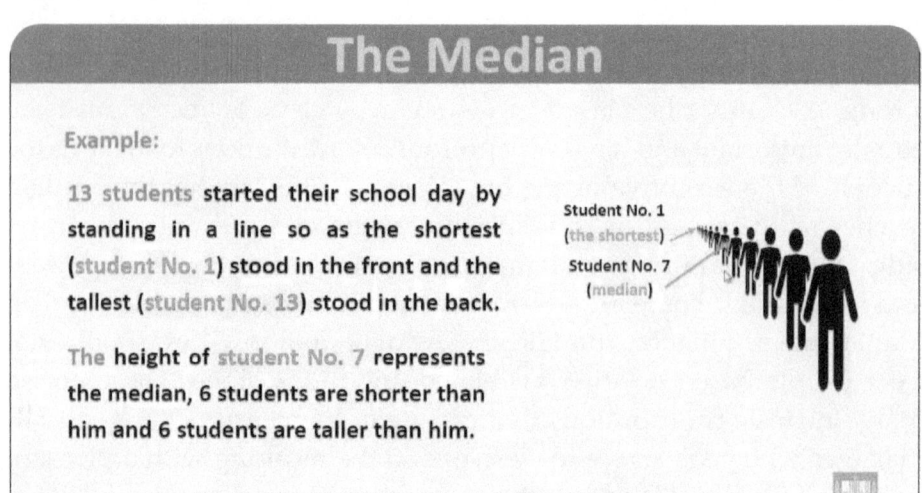

The Median

Example:

13 students started their school day by standing in a line so as the shortest (student No. 1) stood in the front and the tallest (student No. 13) stood in the back.

The height of student No. 7 represents the median, 6 students are shorter than him and 6 students are taller than him.

Student No. 1 (the shortest)
Student No. 7 (median)

Business Development – Thy Name Is Success

I narrate this idea with passion as I realized only late in life what a true Marketing or Business Development function is. I wish I was young and start all over again. But, I know it is not possible but for most of you, this is the time to enlarge your perception of business development. All of us are Marketing people in a way. We have to sell our request for leave. We have to sell our desire to take our family to a picnic. We have to sell our idea to the boss, customers and so on. There is always a role that we understand and play. But, there is a hard core true role which is very profound and relevant. This true role is the essence of the work function that one does and this is what we are going to analyze in the context of Marketing or Business Development. If we look at the role of a marketing team, any one will narrow it down to the following deliverables:

1. Generating a good enquiry
2. Creating a good proposal
3. Getting a good order
4. Managing customer interaction leading to a good relationship

We can add more activities differentiating the sales and marketing functions to this list. But that is not the point. Now, let us look at the same thing mentioned above from a True Role perspective. What is a good enquiry? Is it one that will have a higher probability of getting converted into an order? Is it one that communicates what the customer is expecting from us? Is it one that tells us what the market pulse is currently? Or is it getting into a situation where the customer becomes comfortable to talk to us freely and will engage us with a spirit of working together and not only just finding a method to evaluate what we offer?

What is a good proposal? Is it one which covers all the customer's requirements? Is it one which is complete from all angles? Is it one which conveys to the customer that we have understood his requirement? Or is it the one where the customer starts learning what is best in class and then decides to redefine his requirement from what is the best for him?

What is a good order? Is it one where we get what we have quoted? Is it an opportunity for us to serve the customer? Or is it the one where the customer will certainly and happily pay us without asking and where the customer has empathy towards our service and looks at it as his opportunity to reward us for supporting him?

We can define a good relationship as one where the customer starts thinking and building his business around our competence. It is a relationship in which he respects us and we remain his principal source of strength. Thus, we can conclude that there are only three roles which a Marketing Team should play:

1. Finding a customer who will talk to us with goodwill (sometimes even when there is no need for any product or service) and redefine his expectations based on our knowledge
2. Finding a customer who will pay us happily and be proud about doing so
3. Finding a customer who will build his business around our competence

The future Business Continuity and success for any organization depends on how effortlessly they build this relationship structure with the customer. Obviously, marketing is not the only agency which can make this happen. Marketing has a responsibility in channeling the internal working towards this structure and in elevating themselves as prime business drivers, not just a first level interface with the customer.

The Curious Case of Abnormality

Let us start with a question. Is it normal or abnormal to discuss this topic? What is normal? What is abnormal? I don't know whether the answer is simple enough. Can we say what is not normal is abnormal and what is not abnormal is normal? Who decides this and on what basis do they decide it?

It is clear to me that we should have a clear definition of "normal" or "abnormal" to make a decision. If one knows what is normal, then the abnormal is easy to define and interpret. But in today's context, we have twisted the definition to suit our convenience and based on what we could actually achieve.

Take for instance the following example. When I go to a toilet and find it clean, I feel that I should talk about it to others as though it is abnormal. Do you know that that toilet is very clean? In the Indian context, many of us have never been used to seeing a toilet clean and hence feel that it is abnormal to have a clean toilet. We don't say on a Tuesday morning that it is a Tuesday morning – instead it is taken for granted and is hence normal. But, when we have not been able to find a clean toilet, we have managed to change the definition that an unclean toilet is normal. Also we have got used to it so much that we recognize a clean toilet as an abnormal situation.

I once went to a meeting which was due to start at 10:00 AM. I was there on the dot, but found no one there. It looked like a very abnormal situation to be there on time, so much so, that people talk about punctuality as an abnormal situation. You hear statements like, "That company is very different. They are very punctual!" What should be very normal, such as things like a clean work place, a clean toilet, a punctual organization, responding on time, closing the communication loop, etc., have become abnormal and merit discussion.

■ I Will Make It Happen

It is also said that if over 50% of the world's population speaks English in a particular way, then it is the right way. Can we accept this logic? Is there no absolute definition of the right way? Going by this logic, if we cannot achieve what is considered normal by common sense, then normal becomes abnormal and vice versa. Statistically speaking, if fewer people do a particular thing in a particular way, it has a tendency to be branded abnormal. It is now up to us to decide what we should do with the abnormality and the key to success lies in this understanding. If we think that abnormality has to be made normal without thinking what the right spirit is, we will end up with having a very normal world which could be totally abnormal. Before touching abnormality, let us first recognize and uphold the right spirit of normality and then work on making what is abnormal as normal or what is normal as abnormal. Let us restore the spirit of normality to the definition of normality so that we remain normal people.

The Non-Linear Understanding of Space – A Learning Perspective

It is true that perception has more to do with how you see something rather than what you see. The intent can never be perceived unless it is explained or, in very rare situations, it happens automatically when the chemistry matches. But in most cases, it ends up only as what the person wants to see.

We have all heard of the famous example of a glass half-full versus a glass half-empty as an indicator of perception, and how to look at things positively. It is indeed a beautiful and apt example for this subject. I wish to share a deeper meaning of this example which will give all of us a better and useful insight to prepare ourselves to perceive properly, and with some principles. It is no doubt important to know how you're looking at it – an empty glass or a full glass. Use it as a basis to improve your approach. At the same time, it is very important to know the following

1. What is the content of what is full?
2. What is the quality of the empty space?
3. The dynamism between the two

If you fill yourself with things that are not matters of focus, priority or are not related to your core objective, the fullness is, in a way, empty. Similarly, if in a company, the resources are not fully utilized, it is a very inefficient system. On a national level, it is a colossal loss of wealth.

It is not good to have anything full or empty. There are times when things have to be full. For instance, if you are undergoing a tragic moment, it is better to be fully occupied so that the mind does not get any irrelevant thoughts. When you are seriously thinking or contemplating, it is very important to be fully empty as it allows you a deeper process of reflection.

Many times, the empty side is needed to leverage the full side. For instance, in time management, if you have free time, you can use it to plan the utility of what is already full. If you don't do this, there is a danger that the work will expand and fill the empty side quickly, giving you no time to think. It will also give you a false sense of being busy or occupied. This brings to the forefront the concept that management of full and empty space is essential to get the best out of yourself and your team. This is where the dynamism between the two is relevant.

Physics teaches us that inertia can be managed with external force only. Fortunately for humans, this external force is what is already internally bestowed by God: commitment, determination, discipline, focus and the like. In general, we can change inertia of full and empty in three ways.

The first is to reduce the full: waste elimination, better efficiency, internalization of knowledge, having a system, delegation and such else. This can also be called unlearning or removing the fat from what we already know. Secondly, we can add newer things which increase the full. The quality of this new addition is a function of the efficiency of learning, the objectives or goals that we have set for ourselves and how we leverage the empty space.

Finally, we come to the most interesting aspect of this management of inertia: the modification of space. It is seldom right to have all the full in one place and all the empty in one space. It is far more meaningful to distribute the full and empty so that the efficiency of retrieval is enhanced and the spaces are better used. It is like the 5S of housekeeping. The real beauty is seen when the empty side and the full side are intertwined. This gives us the powerful philosophy of divide and rule. Maturity is when you are able to do this in auto-pilot mode, where things happen in a natural way and at a sub-conscious level. This is also called self-management. The first thing to learn before learning, is how to learn.

The Non-Linear Understanding of Space – A Learning Perspective

Learn To Learn from Everyone and Change At Least One Thing

A wise man once said, "When the student is ready, the teacher will arrive." Can we wait for the student to be ready? Or do we accelerate this process by knowing how a person learns, which is different for different people? When we were kids, and were learning, our teachers and parents found stories to tell us, which would deliver the knowledge. We have not forgotten many of these even now, as the stories ensure that the knowledge remains with us forever. Similarly, in problem-solving, there is a nice concept called QC Story (QC Story is used in depicting Motivating stories of problem-solving. Here QC is Quality Control or Quality Circle). QC Story is a method of communicating knowledge for others to learn, remember and use. But in life, also, there are stories which are generally passed on by word of mouth. It is not for nothing that philosophers state that there is so much to learn from life. The access to these stories is very limited as many people do not seek this form of learning.

I want to start with a statement. Every person we see on the road has a story behind them. Some of these stories are so powerful that we will immediately feel small. I wish to narrate and share two such stories. I was walking in the park and a very elderly man was sitting on a bench and asked me for the time. I told him the time and immediately, true to human nature, assumed–that the poor man couldn't afford a watch. Maybe he had no place to live and was maybe financially weak. It never occurred to me that I was only comparing him with what I knew about myself, and what I did not know about him. Soon, I met my friend and we passed this elderly man again and he asked the time again. This time my friend said, "Uncle! How are you? The time is 5:00 PM. How is everyone at home?" We then walked away after the conversation ended. I asked my friend if he knew the old man. My friend then told me about the man and his story.

Born in a relatively poor family, he had single-handedly educated his siblings and then tragedy struck when their uncle's family lost the uncle. This man took care of their family, as well. He got them all married and managed finances so capably that there was no waste. He ensured that all the people ate well, were educated well, got reasonable medical treatment and settled down in life. I felt small immediately, when I looked at myself. Here I was, struggling to run my company, which on the face of it had better resources. All the principles we were teaching had been practiced by this obscure person – waste management, priority based working, socialism, short and long-term planning, finance management, budgeting, etc.

The second story was even more fascinating. Again, during one of my walks, I met a person I knew. He was well-to-do with an amazing ability to teach and had great stage presence. He was begging near the park. I was so surprised and felt so bad that I stopped by him and asked what had happened and how he reached this state. What he told me was so fascinating that I did not sleep that night. He told that he was breaking his ego. He had everything he needed, but off late, he was getting a larger-than-life feeling and tended not to respect others and tended to have a superiority complex and started looking down on people. He met a guru who told him to do things that he would not do easily. He gave him the first lesson for change. "Go and beg on the streets and see how you feel. You don't need money and you think big of yourself and you wish to change. Try to do this for a week and see the difference."

On my way back home, I felt very heavy when I reflected about myself. Here I was, struggling to change certain aspects of my company. I was finding it so difficult to ask an executive to do a different thing and there I saw a man who was taking so much effort to make a change in himself. I am not advocating that we should beg or do similar things. But it is clear to me that change is like rebirth. Unless you feel the shock, you will not attempt to change. But the easy way to do it is to make a resolution that we will make one change a week from what we have always been doing. Change the route you take to office, change the proposal template, change the payment terms, change the method of teaching, documenting, auditing and so on. Unless we change, we don't see change and we will never know what is better. Kudos and three cheers to life and for every person on the street who has a story! What we don't know is exactly what we should know!

Geometric Progression – The Foundation for a Learning Organization

There are several ways to learn. Many of us learn by accident, which is the most common form. A typical situation is the receipt of a customer complaint or a problem that triggers a set of actions which gives knowledge as a byproduct in the course of resolving the problem. The other form of learning is based on a systematic process where we learn irrespective of the outcome of an event. Simply put, we learn when there is a success or failure. But this is not very common.

It is important to realize that knowing what works is not knowledge, but why it works is knowledge. Knowing why things work is the basis for preventing what does not work. Let us look at the first form of learning, which is based on failure as it is the most common form we see. Success is much sought after. In that, too, the first success is very memorable. It also is to be remembered that the first success need not be the same as the first attempt. Though many people like to succeed in the first attempt, it is worthwhile to examine this a bit more closely so that we can find the best way to get it.

The question to be asked is, is the first success the only criteria that is important or is it the "knowledge of how" we got this first success that is more important? I am sure that all mature people will agree that along with success, it is very crucial to know how and why we succeeded or to know what factors contribute to success and failure. Let us look at geometric progression, to explain this concept. This will explore the probability of first success. Let us take an example. Suppose we got the first success in the fourth attempt, this means we failed in the first three attempts and succeeded in the fourth. Mathematically, if p is the probability of success, then (1-p) is the probability of failure and hence, if we succeeded in the fourth attempt, the probability can be expressed as (1-p) to the power three multiplied by p.

This is a very important formula. Each time (1-p) happens, we have failed. This also means that there is learning. The number of times we have to try before we get the first success depends on the probability of success. If the probability of success is low, we have to try several times and each time we fail, we should learn. This learning will increase the probability of success and hence reduce the number of attempts in future. This is an excellent self-adjusting formula and the world of learning, provided, we learn from failures.

Continuous learning is the process of increasing the probability of success and a learning organization is one which will require fewer and fewer number of attempts for the first success, as it matures. On the other hand, several trials do not reflect effectiveness from a customer's point of view. It is equally important to realize that if we succeed in the first attempt, and we don't know anything about why we succeeded, it is a hollow success, as we will not know when failures will come. Such a blind situation will shatter the customer's confidence as this will be viewed as organizational indifference. A typical example is when a company develops a new product and after its initial approval, faces problems when the part is taken for regular production.

No one wants to have problems. Problems occur because we have not learnt enough. Learning is not a statement which says that we are learning. Learning is a deeper understanding of the scheme of things around us and picking up details which are visible only to those who dare and care to learn, and those who accept sincerely that they don't know something. Accepting that we don't know is the only starting point for learning. Once we taste the pleasure of learning, it is contagious and spreads across the organization, making it a truly learning organization. Let us reflect on this. Remove all the layers of scale that we have accumulated and get into the softer inner core of ourselves and start learning. True knowledge need not be propagated. It beckons everyone who matters to flock around us and radiates a power which is obvious.

Triggering the Trigger – Converting Helplessness into Control

Many people prefer predictable lives where there are no surprises, where everything is planned and goes on as per plan. This is a philosophy and attitude where there is nothing like right or wrong.

But, in a business perspective, we need triggers for action. These triggers are the equivalent of causes which change predictable situations to situations which offer the possibility and excitement of something different happening, about which we don't know.

Let us look at what a trigger means. You are sitting in your seat. Suddenly, the phone rings and after that, a series of actions takes place. A customer walks in to your shop. Then, there is some action. It is not important to know at this point whether the trigger will result in any meaningful result or not. But, it is the opportunity to convert a trigger which is the challenge and the basis for our efforts. That reflects the internal competence of the organization. A successful company is one that learns from both, positive and negative outcomes of the trigger. On the other hand, you see some triggers like this. You are relaxing quietly in your room after a day's work and suddenly, you decide to take a walk (This is a trigger which is difficult to explain). You go on the walk and meet someone on the way and many things start happening after that. These are triggers which come to you.

From a Management perspective, understanding and mastering the signals of a trigger is a key element in success. In the same light, it is equally essential to plant the nucleus for triggers to happen, instead of waiting for triggers to happen in a random manner. Can triggers take place on their own? The answer is both, Yes and No. There are two worlds around the place we live in:

1. The esoteric: The world about which we know very little. It is generally governed by providence. It is difficult to explain why many things happen. These are closer to philosophy, religion and beliefs. These offer – post-event – consolation as a validation and acceptance for what happens. Some refer to this as destiny. But, from a real world point of view, we need more manageable and controllable explanations. It is like a pilot steering an aircraft. No pilot likes to do a blind landing though it is essential sometimes.
2. The exoteric – For want of a better word, I use exoteric for the world which is not esoteric. A world where humans would like to take pride in the result of actions that they have initiated and would like to bask in the glory of satisfaction, which gives them a feeling of superiority. The advantage of an exoteric world is that humans are motivated to get up in the morning with an urge to do something.

Let us get back to the trigger concept. If you follow the esoteric world theory, you are compelled or ready to wait for triggers to happen and justify the lack of success in the lack of triggers. On the other hand, the exoteric world concept gives you a basis for work. Just get into action – the kind of action that is not expecting any results, but is an effort that plants triggers in your zone of influence. Better still, is to start initiating triggers for others to reciprocate with an expectation that the network of triggers will always expand in value and will give you back what you need while giving to others what they need.

Expanding your zone of influence in itself is a long-term trigger. Don't lose an opportunity to meet people, participate in events, travel, get into the social network, do good deeds to anyone you see and to show a genuine interest in everything this world offers and so on. Finally, take the examples of what a concentrated reflector can achieve. By repeated reflections, the intensity of the output is very strong and can do wonders like solar power generation. In the same way, a system of focused triggers reflected several times can generate a power which can be harnessed for all our benefit. Trigger the trigger!

Triggering the Trigger – Converting Helplessness into Control

The Warmth and Wisdom of the Black Sheep

Let's go back to basics – something we learnt in kindergarten: Baa Baa Black Sheep.

But before that, let me narrate an experience. In a program I attended recently, the faculty made a very important point when he was discussing the concept of Economic Value Addition which is the real value the business adds after removing the material cost. The faculty mentioned that the Value Addition made by an employee should fall in three parts, not necessarily equal in proportion:

1. The first portion should go to the company's stakeholders for giving the opportunity to work
2. The second portion should go to the employees and for their welfare
3. The third portion should go to the future generation, i.e., for research and development for sustaining their future.

It made a lot of sense and it looked balanced to me. This investment wisdom was always there, but we never realized it. I will turn your attention now to the kindergarten rhyme:

Baa Baa Black Sheep

Have you any wool

Yes sir, yes sir – Three bags full

One for my master

One for my dame and

One for the little boy who lives down the lane

Here, the wool is the offering by the sheep or in any organization's language, it is the return from the enterprise. What a powerful rhyme! The last three sentences are a direct reflection of the management investment wisdom, which we saw earlier. The reference to the master is a reference to the stakeholders, teachers, parents or company. The reference to the dame is meant to convey ourselves, our well being, family and friends. The reference to the Little Boy living down the lane is the future.

This reference is actually much better than the Management wisdom. The little boy living down the lane can be interpreted as the immediate future, which we will see, and not a very long-term future which would go in circles. If we see the immediate future properly, then the long-term future is only a natural extension.

It is not always finance that can be the beneficiary of this wisdom. Knowledge and competence can also be interpreted with these principles. Any human resource in an organization learns continuously. Apart from the direct use of this knowledge for the business, there is another use for this knowledge, if we convert the learning into internal competence. Again there are three levels of competence which can be derived. The first is the competence which we transfer continuously to the Management to enable them to better manage and control the business.

The second competence is to each individual that builds his ability to learn and adapt. The third competence is to create a structure which enables learning to adapt to the future needs.

India is a land where investments are always encouraged. It is a good practice to invest, once we start earning. But again wisdom directs you to make a balanced investment, which means that you set aside something for the Lord, your parents, or well-wishers for making you what you are. Then, set aside a good portion for yourself and enjoy the life without wasting money. Also, invest something for your learning and development. Lastly, save something for an eventual future requirement which could be retirement, some travel, some unforeseen medical expenses or for developing others who are needy. Doing anything in excess is a useless virtue. Leading a balanced life is an absolute necessity.

As Mahatma Gandhi said, "Nature has enough for a man's need but not for his greed." Learn to differentiate between expenses and investments. Resources have to be allocated properly to ensure that there is no wasteful expenditure such as discussing the same thing again and again. On the other hand, direct your resources towards activities like relationship building, individual development, etc. which can be useful to society.

Manageance – The Vision Centric Dance of the Management

....

Let me introduce a new word in this communication – MANAGEANCE – which is a shortened form of the phrase "Management Dance." We will see an essence comparison with the dance that we know, and see how relevant it is to modern management. There is practically no one who does not enjoy dance. The form of dance may differ, but it is always a pleasure to watch dance, not to mention dancing itself, if one is so gifted. What is it that makes a dance unique?

On first thought, the following two elements of a dance stand out as significant:

1. The rhythmic pattern accompanied by the body expression
2. The message or story that is conveyed

Every dance has a theme or a story to convey. This is done through a combination of a rhythm, an expression using the body and many times accompanied by light and sound effects. In India, most of the dance conveys some form of religious message or story. When I look closely at dance and management, I see a very unique relationship. In any organization we also have two significant elements, namely:

1. The vision or purpose of the organization
2. The service which is offered through its various manifestations

Many times, people in the organization forget the vision and focus just on the service. If the service does not effectively convey the organizational vision, the outside world, most importantly, the customers don't get to know the real purpose of the company that they are dealing with. Every aspect of the organization's service should portray the vision of the company. Just like in dance, we have to use the various elements that we have in an organization like structure, people, systems and processes and so on to this effect.

Dance is further exemplified when we look at the stage, lighting, music and the energy level in the performance. We can broadly summarize two types of dance performances:

1. A dance which just about conveys the story and gives a minimum satisfaction to the viewer
2. A passionate dance with the right amount of energy and adaptation which gives the thrill and near-certain power transferred to the audience to carry them along and make a dent in their lives.

Energy and adaptation are two key elements that make a dance relevant even after several years. The same logic applies to organization which has to be relevant even in the future with a different set of expectations. As long as the service offered is adapted to future needs, and the right amount of energy is visible, the organization will always be relevant. Both, energy and adaptation are functions of management guidance.

Vision is the story and the product or service is the expression. To this, we add the support systems we have, such as people, culture, processes, method of getting things done, energy levels and the right orientation – and we have a dance that attracts the world that is targeted by the organization to remain with them forever.

The divine dance of the gods, the near divine dance of the mortals like us and the Manageance, the dance of the Management, are religions by themselves. The benefactors of such religions patronize the organization in good and bad times. The solace they get dealing with an organization performing the right Manageance is par description.

Manageance – The Vision Centric Dance of the Management

The Leadership Challenge – Maybe This Is the Story of Your Company

Here is a recipe for destroying a good business concept through time and innocently through perceived smartness. Sometimes in life, someone comes in with a wonderful idea to start a business. The idea is unique and the founder dares to deviate from the standard path. The business is conceived around the brilliance of the concept and not on price. The service offered is unique and has all the flavor of ingenuity and the pleasure is purely in the delivery of the service and watching the satisfaction of the customer. The organization is built around this principle and the people are molded likewise.

The business thrives as the customer has never tasted such a service at that point in time and there is all-round growth. Then, smartness sets in. Someone internal to the organization or someone external, who has been impacted by this concept, thinks that it is time to make it easy for the customer and make it a much bigger business, an innocent and smart idea. But, the game plan is not smart, although it appears so. The new business, in a way, competition, starts packaging a different service which cuts the essential elements of the original concept and puts price in the forefront.

It is not difficult to convince gullible customers about the modified approach and another nucleus is created. Then, further mutation starts. Gradually, we have different versions of the original concept, each one putting price in the front and a package which ensures poorer service in design and delivery. This leads to a mushroom of service providers, all genuinely believing in what they do but without any understanding of the truthfulness of the original concept. Then, everyone is impacted. With time, different survival modes are adopted. Some survive and some vanish.

Now let us look at the original organization which started the concept. They have two choices

1. To fall in line with the rest and perish.
2. To stick to their concept but innovate.

The choice is clear if we wish to survive. But there is going to be a lot of internal pressure. Let us look at one such internal pressure. There is a situation where clients are ready to come to this company provided the price is at par with the rest. Again, the company has two choices:

1. Take it at a low cost.
2. Leave the business.

It is easy to run away from the business. But, it is smarter to take the client as it ensures that the opportunity remains. Here is where innovation is crucial. But after taking the client, the company always invariably makes the following mistakes:

1. Assign this business a low priority.
2. Offer a poor service – under the low cost argument.
3. Delegate this client to less competent personnel.

This is not exhaustive, there are many more. All these form a sure recipe for death of the business, whereas the smartest thing to do would have been to:

1. Assign a high priority in the hope that this client can be converted into a loyal and permanent long-term customer.
2. Involve the most competent people to change the mindset of the customer to respect the service.
3. Create a unique interpretation of the benefit of the service and make the customer taste it.
4. Create in the minds of the client a respect for the organization and its vision.
5. Support the client in improving their business and look for long-term opportunities.

This very much depends on the strength and conviction of the vision of the original concept. This is a leadership test and the next step depends on the people who are spearheading the business. The writing

■ I Will Make It Happen

is clear on the wall on what should be done. After all, survival is not compulsory.

Give Me the Right Speed and I Will Give You the Right Compliance

Many organizations have clearly adopted the systems route for running their business and their focus has been the Design and Implementation of good systems. Adequacy and compliance are two pillars that can lead to effectiveness of systems. We have discussed a lot on compliance in this book. In this segment, I wish to share a different perspective on adequacy. Most of us would have understood adequacy of the system requirements as expected by the various standards. Some would have gone a bit ahead and looked at technical adequacy aspect as well.

Now, let us look at another aspect which is at the core of the design of a system and in a large way this aspect drives the psychological aspect of compliance. This aspect is speed. Every system has speed. For instance, the rate of issue of a PO, the rate of clearance of incoming goods, the rate of production, the rate of raising invoice and so on. Speed is very much a design element and not something which comes on its own. Mostly we don't pay attention to the rate of doing an activity when we design and document a system. Perhaps we leave it assuming that it will happen automatically.

Now, let us see the implication of speed of system on the psychology of compliance. Every organization has a speed which is dictated by its vision for growth and demands of customers. If the system speed does not match with the speed of the organization, we have two types of errors:

1. Type 1 – If the organization speed is more than system speed, there is a tendency to deviate from the system. For example, people jumping into bus by not adhering to any queue if the

frequency of bus is lower than the speed with which people come to the bus station.

2. Type 2 – If the system speed is more than the organizational speed, there is a lethargy which creeps in and there is tendency to bunch activities together and do it as per convenience and not need. For example, the bus does not depart on time if the frequency of buses is more than the speed with which people come to the bus- station.

These two types of error are at the root of the psychology behind system compliance. Lack of understanding of this psychology can lead to erroneous conclusion and a poor attribution to people's attitude – convenient judgment – as the root cause of system non-compliance. Let us look at any internal system like raising of a Purchase Order or the issue of an Order Acceptance.

If the speed of raising a Purchase Order is lower than the organization speed, then the following types of errors are sure to occur:

a. There is a tendency to deviate from the procedural steps – more by people in authority
b. There is a tendency to jump the sequence of actions and an individual dominance is seen
c. There is a tendency to disregard the interface functions and other functions are taken for granted
d. There is a poor interpretation of "How customer is more important than system" and this message is carelessly thrown around

It is never the people at lower levels who deviate from the system. It is always the people in authority who set the trend and then chaos sets in when others take their own share of interpretations. What is actually needed is to look at the system and make it compatible speed-wise with the organization and one will never see non-conforming systems. In fact, a slightly higher speed from the organization will motivate people to improve their efficiency and innovation to better the system as they see the opportunity to stretch themselves and comply.

It is always true that all instances of non-conformances are almost always because of design.

Give Me the Right Speed and I Will Give You the Right Compliance

The Deceptive Practice of Becoming God with the Help of Probability

God: a question in the minds of a lot of people for ages. Some feel that God is within us. Some look upwards for a possible glimpse of god. Most of us practice a lot of rituals in the hope of meeting God in this life or reaching God after this life. And, we also see a very different practice in our day-to-day lives. We see so many of us assuming the position of God or getting into a belief that we are God with a little support from probability.

How does this happen and what is the role of Probability?

Probability is the chance of an event happening. We all want favorable events to happen. When this happens, there are smiles. When it happens again, confidence starts building. When this happens repeatedly, confidence is strengthened. When this happens continuously for a long time, the confidence slowly transforms into arrogance when we take responsibility for this success or attribute this success to ourselves.

Take my example. When I get a headache, somewhere, since I learnt that a particular pill helps, I take that pill and my headache vanishes. When this happens repeatedly, when probability of success is high, I tend to assume the position of God and start attributing this to my great knowledge. Let us assume that at some point, the headache does not go away with a pill, I get worried not about the headache, but about the threat to my position as God and start doing aggressive actions more to protect my position till I realize that I have to turn to GOD.

Let us take a company making a Business Plan. They achieve their planned targets. Their confidence increases and they draw up a second plan and assume that they succeed again. Now, they start believing in all those things which they are not actually capable of, not knowing the power of providence and in a short time frame, they assume the position of God – Yes! We can achieve anything with our planning process. All is well till there is a failure. Initial reactions are always protection of their position as God and not acceptance of the problem or learning. They look for innovative reasons which push their comfort level around the position of God. Once the probability gets lowered further which means they see more failures, they turn to God.

In review meetings too, the top management starts attributing success to their power of guidance, communication or motivation. The first signs of failure are never used for learning as the management is more battling their threatened position of being GOD.

Eventually, we all learn. I realize that there are several factors for my headache. The business planning people understand that their Business Plan can go for a toss by an activity in a totally unrelated area like a bombing in another country which has cascading effect on customer confidence leading to a failure of their Business Plan. The top management realizes that motivation and communication are just catalysts but the real strength lies in predicting the unknown.

It is not out of place to mention a famous preaching by Deming. The most important knowledge for a management to succeed is either unknown or unknowable. Under this circumstance the only role for all of us is to keep known things under control as much as possible so that the probability of success is maintained. Nevertheless, all things eventually do change forcing us to face failures and then only the learning process starts. We don't realize at that time the fact that we are actually improving the probability of success by learning. Learning is the key and not assuming the position of God by attributing success to one's efforts. The only aspect worth doing is the effort itself with unmatched devotion.

What an irony!

Humans start as children and respect God. As they grow they gain experience. Then they start theorizing with experience. Based on the probability of success for their theory, they tend to become God or assume the position of God and start attributing several qualities which they don't actually have for themselves. This manifests as arrogance so

■ I Will Make It Happen

much so that there is a tinge of assumption of a position bigger than GOD itself. When failure starts happening, initial reactions are more to protect the position of God but when problems persist, they ultimately turn to the actual GOD and say, "Oh God! Please help me!" Then, they start learning and improving the probability of success.

Man asks God, "Am I wrong in assuming that I am right?"

God answers, "Yes you are right in assuming that you are wrong."

God, are you listening?

> **MATTHEW 22:29**
>
> ✦ "Jesus replied, 'You are in error because you do not know the Scriptures or the power of God.'" (NIV)

My Dear Energy – You Are Useful and Beautiful

Energy is very nice to have and can do a lot of things. But, it has to be managed. A lot of this energy is visible to us when we see kids playing, salespeople chasing customers, production teams chasing targets, management chasing the expectations of the stake holders, people organizing events and so on. One important task for any management is to provide such organizational opportunities to use this energy. As long as a human being is positive, this energy is renewable and the quality of such renewed energy is better than the previous one.

But this is not all. There is a lot of invisible energy which gets built up inside, and does not get an outlet to escape. Such energy has a good potential for use but more important is the fact that this energy is also dangerous if not used and not dissipated properly. When a superior talks rough to a subordinate, a lot of energy is built inside the subordinate. We can see several examples of such energy getting built when there is organization bias or unfairness, local politics, work environment not healthy, disparity between colleagues, responsibilities to be executed without authority, targets to be achieved without adequate resources and so on.

This is a lot of energy that is waiting to explode. Many times the explosion does not take place openly but it manifests in several ways like a coldness in the relationship, lower efficiency, impoliteness in communication, poor response to customer needs, building of chimneys, finding ways to prove that things will go wrong, outbursts in family and society, risky driving and so on. All this leads to self-destruction.

It is one thing to ensure that such energy does not get built up. But in a growing organization, there can be several opportunities where unintentionally events take place which create such energy build-up.

Hence, it is the task of every individual in the organization to find sustainable ways to dissipate this energy. There are three factors which are important while planning and executing this dissipation:

1. The time that is spent
2. The management of the gradient
3. Allowing pores to open so that some natural corrections take place.

The time that is to be spent is an art in judgment. It has to be a certain minimum to ensure that the intentions are right and not done mechanically. Too much of time will lead to wrong conclusions like someone is trying to patch up. Think of an ocean. When there is enough space, the water hits the shore beautifully giving a visual treat.

Gradient is dependent on the time. If we have less time, we have to manage a steeper gradient. It also depends on the amount of energy that is built. One idea is to do this regularly so that there is no elevation in energy levels. The communication should be systematic and step by step so that we don't fall off. Typical example is when we climb down a steep staircase: we do it with great care.

In this process, we should consciously allow small and appropriate "give and take" where there is a mix of emotions in the mind of the individual managed and the person can use this for future bonding. Open up wounds – but not too much to damage self respect, but at the same time good enough for natural treatment or further assisted treatment.

As a fair extension, we can use this principle even to enhance the quality of good energy that is built through constructive means like conduct of training programs, management reviews, sales meets, etc. After the conclusion of the activity, allow some time to take care of the three things we mentioned above. Do not end anything abruptly. Ensure that there is a good amount of energy at manageable levels left with the individuals when they leave such events. A rough sea is a beauty if we can manage it. Otherwise, the energy has to be dissipated to make it smoother like a nice beach where the water gently breaks. There is energy even then. But the art of management is to manage the energy to distinguish between roughness and beauty.

My Dear Energy – You Are Useful and Beautiful

Compliance Is the Non-Negotiable First Step for Improvement

We all know the importance of compliance in the implementation of any system. Though it is the culmination of all our efforts, it can hardly be branded as the end of the process. On the contrary, we say it is only the beginning.

Why is it the beginning?

Let us look at the following statement.

"If you have a system, you must follow. If, for some reason, you cannot follow the system, change it. If you are unable to change it, then follow it. But don't break the system. Breaking the system is a crime as it makes others suffer more than what the person has gained by breaking the system."

Further, the person demonstrates several negative features in one stroke: cowardice, lack of commitment, lack of sensitivity to the needs of other members of the system, a total disrespect for the system itself and a lack of faith on the ability of a system to provide an unbiased work environment." The list can go on. Compliance bridges a very important gap between theory and practice. We have a lot of good plans and a lot of dreams, and we take extra care to define the path. Unless we move on this path, we don't know whether the path made by us is worthy of movement.

Even to know whether something is good or bad, we have to first comply. Instead of sitting on the fence and making statements or analyzing things hypothetically, it is better to first walk the talk to know whether the road exists in the intended manner, whether it is worth making a trip and above all it does lead us to our objectives or goals. Compliance with a system gives a very powerful feedback on two aspects:

1. The adequacy and effectiveness of the system or the lack of it
2. The pleasure or pain encountered while following the system

Both of these are very important for any individual. The first strengthens the ability of a person to progressively de-skill any job and create proven methods for success. The second strengthens the motivation of a person in increasing the faith in this approach. The combination of these two benefits is the creation of an improvement engine. The engine that uses the creative ability of a human being in finding a solution to solve the fluctuating vagaries of attitude of a human being. This is a classic example of a human being developing competence to improve the result of a human being's competence. Let us continue this topic to see a few more insights into this beautiful concept called – compliance.

From a purely human perspective, there is a need to buy-in support for any system. This compliance cannot be enforced – though initially we may have to gently coerce people to move in this direction. For long-term sustained compliance, we have to understand human psychology.

There are four emotions within a human being that have to be addressed properly for getting long-term buy-in support through natural compliance. There is no need to stress that compliance has to be natural. It has to be the most natural thing to do, like getting up and walking. It is not out of place to mention that there is a lot of contribution from a system design perspective to make compliance natural. Any other alternate to complying with this system should be more difficult. In other words, compliance to a system should be the easiest thing to do. All these explanations will not make a person comply unless we address the four emotions:

1. A sense of excitement
2. The elimination of apprehension
3. The joy of seeing the objectives being met
4. The sarcasm

In a way all of these are related. Let us look at each of these things. Excitement is absolutely necessary when we try a new system. There should be a certain thrill when we follow a system. This thrill can also be in the form of a subtle doubt: What will happen if I follow? Will this actually work? When I comply, will the next step automatically fall in place? All these are instances of excitement. An example can be a click sound when an interlock or mistake proofing takes place.

Everyone has apprehensions. They are alright within their comfort zone. The status quo will be preferred to any change. Thus, it is important that people are adequately informed or communicated to before launching a system. Leadership of a system is achieved when everyone in the system has to follow the system. Seeing is believing, and is also a key factor to alleviate fear. When everyone is following, all apprehensions are set to rest.

Nothing succeeds like success. If we don't achieve the objectives, no one will respect the system. More importantly, people should not see any other alternative as a better way of doing a certain thing. This calls for a lot of smart thinking by the designers of the system. An example can be completing a task in the fastest possible time due to compliance. Lastly, everyone feels that they are different and all this will not work. They also feel that they are better than the system. This is the starting point for non-conformance. But fortunately, everyone remains on the border initially, and hence, it is easy to overcome this problem. This manifests in so many ways. I will not be the first, let me see others, this will work for a short term only and hence I will follow my own rules and so on. But sarcasm will go away when they actually comply.

There is a big potential difference between complying and not complying. The moment you comply the mind set changes to a positive state and everything will be viewed positively. That is why we say the first step is to comply. All the walls built around a human being vanish when the person starts to comply. It is amazing but true. But the start of compliance is just the beginning. If simultaneously excitement comes in and the apprehensions go away, the sarcasm will vanish. People with sarcasm will ultimately become the brand ambassador for the system if we work on this emotion.

A final word. The best system is one where the system itself ensures compliance and there is no need for any outside authority to enforce compliance. Think of the human body. It is the best example of how all systems rally round to support compliance. For the human body, patience is needed and the natural design of the body gets rid of any intruder to the system. When we don't have patience, we go to the doctor. Then we force a lot of system bypass in the name of medicines and quick cure and do more damage in the long run. Comply first, gain confidence, rally support from other members of the system, together expel any intruder and ensure compliance in a positive and natural manner.

The Shame of Putting the Hands Up and Head Down

"It is so simple to be happy, but it is very difficult to be simple." This is a fine dialogue from *Baawarchi*, an old Indian movie. It is a thought-provoking statement which lies at the heart of ISR, i.e., an Individual's Sharing Responsibility. We have all heard of Corporate Social Responsibility (CSR). On par with it, ISR is important as it hits at a fundamental responsibility for any individual to express his views clearly and when it is needed. By using the word responsibility, we are not suggesting an optional need, but rather, demanding definite action.

Simplicity is not about the way we project ourselves or the way we live, but more about the way we think. Simple thinking is a stress-buster and a health tonic. Simple thinking manifests in the form of simple actions, which are pure and from the heart, and have no complicated expectations attached. They are natural and spontaneous. What is natural and spontaneous is from God and has the most intrinsic worth or value.

If this is so, why do people avoid speaking up or expressing their views? Is it that they don't have a point of view when a point is being discussed? Is it a cultural trap of "don't talk" when there is a hierarchy in existence? Is it that people simply don't care? I don't know. I did not recognize the importance of this requirement until I got involved with various people in various meetings from various organizations, including mine.

It is not just disabled or challenged people who are helpless. Support is needed by everyone, more so in Management. As a matter of fact, in management, there are several platforms available or created for the objective of getting support. Some examples are one-to-one discussions, review meetings, informal meetings, and formal meetings and in the email world, it is through the art of marking people on copy or blind copy. Support does not mean getting an affirmative response always. Support is also in hearing the negative, or a different perspective. By not responding at all, we are only communicating a total lack of involvement and interest.

Good kings in the past had advisers who had the task of analyzing and guiding the king. Today's management is not very different. Today, management is not just one person at the top. Management exists at all levels and the organization's needs are very complex, because knowledge and information are scattered across several layers of an organization. Great organizations build their managerial talent by getting people to soak in the company's vision and to use their senses to review all words, actions, policies, initiatives, aspirations, strategies and such else, and then evaluate them against the company's vision. Overall, it is about what is right, and then, about guiding each other in taking the path that is respected, effective, valuable and worth moving along.

No one is perfect. A position is not an indicator of knowledge or wisdom. Just like it is humility to seek advice it is also a responsibility to give advice.

Many times, I have seen people accepting the words of hierarchy, and later, when they are outside, they discuss vociferously among their colleagues saying that something the hierarchy said would not work. Sometimes, they come through a roundabout way to say this. "I wanted to mention this in the meeting, but I did not want to be wrongly interpreted. The actual problem is…"

When you ask for an opinion, the head must be held high, the mind must be simple, the motive must be genuine, the expectations should be pure and the hand must go up. It is a shame to lift the hand up while the head is bent down. The magnetic field in the organization should be such that there is a free flow of original views which collectively has the power to build a fiber which is strong and has the stamp of collective approval so that the organization marches into its survival battle with such a source of internal competitive strength. The basic qualities that we have to develop or nurture are: a genuine interest, a thorough involvement, a well-read or informed state, a clear acceptance of the company's vision, a detailed awareness of the current situation

■ I Will Make It Happen

or matter under discussion, a systematic thinking process, an ability to critically review and the final unambiguous expression of one's view. A wise man once said, "If I give you a rupee and you give me back a rupee, there is no gain or loss. But if I give you an idea and you give me back an idea, we now have two ideas."

Let us follow the famous dictum: "Where the head is held high and will remain high always."

HEAD DOWN, HANDS UP

The Several Faces of One at a Time

Life is a great teacher. Instead of judging our various experiences from our very limited interpretation of what is happening, we should systematically learn from the experiences. The progression from being childish to being ambitious to being mature to being calm is as amazing as life itself.

Let us look at ambition and maturity. Ambition brings with it a certain degree of impatience and the drive to do several things while we are alive. Then, we make two mistakes. The first mistake is related to ambition. We multiply the outcome of every idea several times to get an indication of our value or wealth to be generated along with an estimate of the time that would be needed to achieve this. The second mistake is related to impatience. We decide that the time to be taken is too long and therefore we have to do several things at a time. Both of these won't be mistakes if we know how to execute the actions correctly.

Most of us then start to do several things at a time. All goes well till we find that reality is not what we thought it was. Soon, we realize that there are several things initiated which are at various stages of completion. Impatience comes up again and we try to take short cuts and then realize that nothing moves. Finally, wisdom prevails when we decide that we have to complete something at least. Then, we narrow it down further to realize that it is better to complete one thing at a time rather than have several things open.

It is at this point that we are ready, mentally and experience wise, to accept "One at a Time" as a great virtue. It is not a new idea and the writing was always clear on the wall. But each of us has to undergo the cleaning process to fully accept this concept. That is why we started with the point – life is a great teacher. One at a time has several virtues. The key among these are:

1. Completion
2. Evaluation and Review
3. Learning

Anything that is completed is a success story and acts as a motivator to take the next action. A completed action is a demonstrated model for others to follow. Once completed, we can evaluate the result and the processes adopted. We can check how it compares with what we set out to achieve in the first place. Again, a completed action is the best candidate for a review. This review is at the heart of learning, which we should use to be more efficient and effective subsequently. The more we are able to rotate this cycle; the better is the all-round learning which we call wisdom. This learning is worthless if it does not help us realize our ambitions by controlling the impatience.

Strength lies in breaking the overall project into several steps which can be implemented one at a time. We should develop the ability to visualize, break it into smaller steps and have a killer instinct to execute each action completely and thoroughly. Once we have this competence, doing more things is only a matter of speed. Speed is not related to doing several things at a time but to rally around a team where each does one thing at a time. The cumulative effect is the speed which was at the root of our impatience. Speed is only relevant if the direction and focus are right.

Ambition, a demonstrated competence to execute and speed in the right direction is a combination, which is a legacy. It should be inherited by the future generation.

Good Is Many Times Better Than Best – Absolute versus Relativity – A Perspective

Absolute versus relative is ultimately the difference between excellence and competition. Many times, we discuss seriously about making improvements, but these discussions convey nothing. For instance, we discuss quality problems and mention that the rework is much better now than last year. We say that our profitability has improved a lot, or I am two inches taller than my sister is.

All these are true in their own ways, and convey a lot in relative terms. But there is nothing of value when we have no idea of the absolute position – for example, improvement in profitability from 2 % to 8 % or from 30 % to 36 %. In most cases, relativity has no meaning unless we know the absolute. If we say we are better or we say something is the best, we ask, "Better among what?" and "Best among what?" This brings a certain comparison among several things and this naturally means that it may not be the very best.

In contrast, good is always good in its truest sense. It need not have comparative value. For instance, blue is not better than red. Blue is good, and so is red. It is good in its own right and existence. True goodness leads to excellence. It brings out the good in relation to good itself.

Similarly, when someone says something is great, it conveys greatness in an absolute sense. But if we say greater, it automatically means that there is something less great and consequently, something else can be greater. If we say greatest, it has a certain finality which is always doubtful and hence conveys greatest among something. This implies that there could be something else which is not included and the search for a better great or a best great will go on. On the contrary, great conveys absolute greatness, great in its own sense. The same is true with standing tall versus taller or tallest.

When you look at comparative terms like better or best, we look at a sort of competition and our efforts are focused on becoming better or the best in that category. Consequently, there is a danger of not going deep into ourselves to bring out our true potential which is good, great or tall. There can be arguments that better at least gives a benchmark target to work towards. But this benchmark orientation puts a lot of strain on the process we use to reach the benchmark, which is not always truly balanced between what is right and wrong. Whereas, when you look towards being good, you look at good from a genuine good point of view, and use all means which are at the heart of being good or great and hence, this brings out excellence. Success is not only determined by competition, but is determined by being relevant, always. Greater or greatest are all acceptable only if the pressure of being greater or greatest does not destroy the process adopted to be greater or greatest. On the other hand, the process of being great will always be good, as it has no pressure of comparison and it has only the genuineness of being good and great. This will always keep the process intact and the end result will be always great and relevant at all times, which is success.

Competition is good only if it brings the right process. Otherwise, competition does more damage. On the other hand, excellence is all-round, both in results and efforts. Don't compete, but excel!

People Who Cannot Stand On Their Own Legs Deserve neither a Standing nor Legs

This is as much applicable to organizations as it is applicable to individuals. First, let us start with appreciating what a standing is. We are not referring to the physical side, although it is very important when we grow. In this context, standing is positioning. Great leaders like Vivekananda, Mother Teresa, Gandhiji and Abraham Lincoln were people with great standing, and their position is relevant even today.

We are not referring to any specific knowledge or expertise when we look at standing. We are looking at generic qualities like being ethical, righteous, preaching good, serving people with no expectations and the like. These are positions worth standing for. We must all create a position for ourselves – in our own way.

Incidentally such positions have made many organizations relevant and successful even today. True success of an enterprise is not in making profits, but in using proper means to make profits. These proper means are being referred to as standing or position. Once the base for a good standing is established, it is also very important to be able to stand on our own legs. Own legs here means the power of conviction and the strength to face all odds while establishing our standing. Support from others is essential but they must be eventually internalized – otherwise it will be very hollow and will collapse when adverse situation demand a bold and assertive decision.

It is always easy to talk of a good standing when things are going fine. The real test comes when we face difficulties or even acute illness. It is said that the true color of a person is known when he gets angry. Likewise, the true strength of our legs is known when we face a difficult situation. The legs must also be capable of steering us away from potentially dangerous situations which will affect our standing.

Just like legs are physically needed for any person to stand, the power of conviction is the most important strength for safeguarding our standing. In an organization, the legs are the collective outcome of the people's convictions and their internal process of thinking, communicating and working. The crucial strength of the physical legs is in the way the joints and muscles are positioned. In a similar manner, the interface in an organization is a crucial contributor to the strength of an organization's legs. It is our collective responsibility to strengthen our individual convictions along with extended coverage to include the entire interface between various functions.

Just like we understand that the strength of a system is in its weakest link, it is always the interface which is the weakest link and their strength determines the sustainability of our standing. Be strong individually, preach the spirit of strength and extend it seamlessly into the interface and we have a strong foundation to stand tall.

What Is Fundamentally Wrong Need Not Go Further Wrong

How many times have we looked at things which have gone wrong, and concluded that it is a consequence of the approach by others? In this message, I wish to draw your attention to how wrong we are.

There are certain natural theories such as, what is fundamentally wrong will tend to be wrong fully and continue to be wrong. For example, if a company decides to implement a System Standard purely for certification, it will invariably end up getting just a certificate and no benefits from the system. It started with a wrong premise and the end result is wrong as long as there is no benefit from the implemented system. It also creates further wrongs. Some of these include the Management thinking that it knows how to run the business of fooling the customer. Sometimes the employees may think that these standards are an eye-wash and are meant to maintain records. The whole atmosphere casts a poor image of the people involved, all of whom are professionals and individually have great accomplishments to their credit but still end up at the bottom of the pile.

Implementing SPC without ensuring a stable process is another example of a wrong which is fundamental. Any efforts put on estimation of the process capability and control will yield no benefits and will result in having a non-value added SPC on the floor. This does not mean that anything which is fundamentally right will eventually end up right although it has a greater chance of being right. Take for example, Customer Focus. If the management team is highly customer focused and adapts itself to the needs of the customer, it has a greater chance of getting the benefit of such an approach, most probably not in the short run but definitely in the long run.

Or is this true?

Maybe we are missing something. What we are missing, is the approach. The approach has to be right. What is meant by the right approach?

When you speak to people, give them the true motivation to remain focused. Ensure that people are trained properly. Emphasize on the need to follow the process. Be fair to all concerned. These are some examples of Right Approach. Even if the objective is fundamentally right, the approach also has to be right and consistently right. We should not forget that we are dealing with people and consistency or as Deming says – Constancy of Purpose – is a very key psychological element which wins people to your side.

Let us explore this to a situation where the objective was fundamentally wrong. Can a Right Approach change something? Fortunately, the answer is yes.

Take for instance the example of a company planning to go for a System Standard certification purely for the sake of the certificate. The consultant hired for this purpose, need not assume that role, even though the contract is intended to get certified. He can do right things like talking to the Senior Management and developing a style by which he shows them how to get real benefits from the system. Try and demonstrate a few benefits and then gradually change the mindset of the customer. This is the right approach. From where the customer started, the consultant can convince him and make him change. In a way, he is God, or assumes the role of God and changes what was fundamentally wrong and take the customer in the path of what is right.

Many customers respect people who stand by what is right even if they unknowingly encourage you to be wrong. The power of being right and the gentle manner in which right things are demanded are abilities and competences that we have to build. This depends on our own understanding of what is right and our conviction on what we know, teach and guide.

This is a commitment to be preached like a religion. A wrong start can be made a right end by adopting the right approach. A right start can end up right only by a right approach. So, what is the deal? The least risk option is to be right in our approach always and have the courage to face any obvious motivation to stray from this path. The wrong gets defeated by the right and the right continues to glow and spread light everywhere.

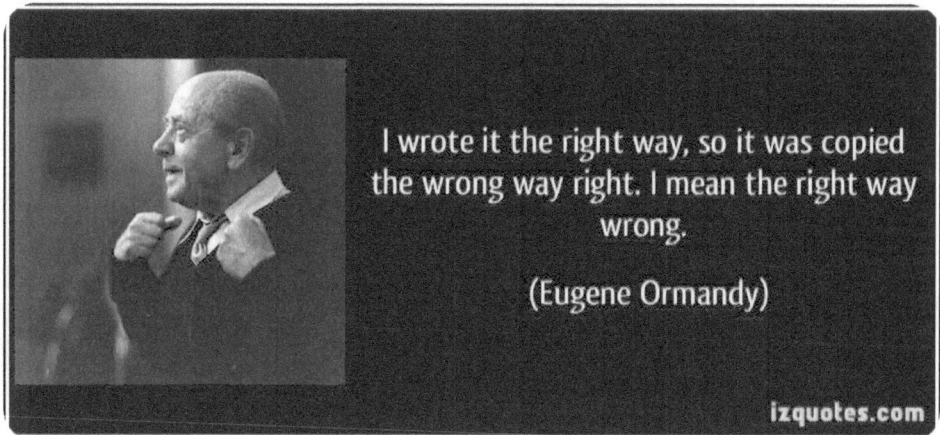

CALMNESS CAN DEFEAT ANYTHING

I wish to present to all of you the Power of Calmness, as I see it. The word calmness itself is the best expression to describe the spirit of calmness. By just reflecting on this word, you should be able to experience certain calmness. We know and have experienced that a very excited person is characterized by a higher heartbeat which affects his judgment. He is hence prone to make mistakes. In fact, a very effective strategy in negotiation is to make your opponent excited or angry, and thus increase their chances of making a blunder. You can win if you learn to be calm. As a natural extension, you can always win and make others win if you can spread calmness.

Any excitement is similar to an increase in the Center of Gravity. We all know from Physics that the higher the Center of Gravity, the lower the stability. You can easily dislodge any object which has a high Center of Gravity. Consequently, the most stable positions are when the Center of Gravity is close to the ground.

Look at the following example from your own life! Sitting, lying down or sleeping postures have the lowest centers of gravity. When you go to a doctor, the doctor asks you to sit down or lie down, and then, he asks the questions. You are in the best position to answer correctly and clearly when you are lying down or sitting down. When you are disturbed or ill, you are waiting to lie down. You are very comfortable, then, to relax, think and decide. Also, the reverse is true. While you are lying down and a certain disturbing thought comes to mind, you sit up or get up. This is the reflex and an automatic increase in the Center of Gravity. These are lessons from nature.

Improving Calmness is similar to lowering of the Center of Gravity. One way of improving calmness is to focus and concentrate. Some people take the help of professionals in learning this – example meditation courses. When we concentrate, we are channeling our energy on a few things instead of allowing our mind to jump on several things. When our mind is hyper active, the Center of Gravity goes up. So, the key is concentration.

To have effective concentration, one can close his eyes or listen to music – both of which have the effect of seeing less or hearing less. That makes your mind calm down. You can see from your own experience that we tend to close the door when we want to concentrate. But ultimately, the real success comes when you are able to concentrate while you are amidst the center of action and not withdraw to get the power of concentration to become calm.

Calmness is contagious. When you learn to be calm and demonstrate calmness, you create the environment for others to follow. Even when a fellow colleague is excited and rushes to you to discuss a disturbing situation, ask him to first sit down, drink water, enquire general things and then get into the subject. You will radiate calmness around you and it will be imbibed by others too.

In business calmness can be interpreted as follows. When a process is stable or in statistical control, the normal distribution is similar to being calm. Assignable causes are forces which raise the Center of Gravity. A documented system has the same effect as creating the environment for calmness. Consequently, compliance with rules and procedures is the same as creating calmness. You can thus interpret calmness in your work and be a focus point for being a messenger of calmness and destroy anything in the way which affects calmness, all the time with a smile and a serene and composed appearance.

May the strength of calmness flow to all of you!

■ I Will Make It Happen

How Much Roundness Should A Round Tolerate?

It is amazing how various real life objects teach us on life and attitudes, if only we look! I am taking one such object – the round, or the sphere. Mathematically, we know that the sphere is a very unique object as it occupies the least total surface area. The surface of a sphere is best appreciated when it is smooth like in a ball. There is a size for the sphere and there is also some content in the sphere.

Let us imagine that the content is the sum total of all our maturity, competence, ego, prejudices and what not. That represents us. The size of the round is similar to the extent of our content. It does not mean that a higher size means a better personality. It has to be also the quality of the content. The roundness around the sphere is the outer shell we have. It is also the amount of resistance we have for anything new. If there is a good and smooth roundness, the surface does not offer grip and as a human being, we should not be so slippery that no one can approach us. We have to be approachable. This approachable nature offers the other person a grip to tag on to you and communicate. Having a perfect roundness is not a healthy configuration.

Further, the surface should not remain smooth and round forever. Then, it is impervious and offers tremendous resistance to any learning. This is also similar to the attitude of Status Quo.

If there is a status quo attitude, then there is no possibility of a change and hence there is no improvement. To get out of status quo, we need to shake ourselves once in a while by exposing ourselves to learning. This is similar to making a small scratch or dent in the roundness of our sphere. The scratch or cut should last just long enough for us to release some of the unwanted constituents in the sphere and add good and noble attributes inside. Then, the scratch or dent should heal like a skin which heals when we get a cut. The frequency of this cut and the depth or exposure depends on your humility, level-headedness and

■ I Will Make It Happen

soon. If the cut is too deep for it to heal quickly, there is a chance that we get into an unstable situation and may get lost. So, a healthy balance is needed and that depends on the strength of our personalities.

Some of us are lucky. By nature, we get an opportunity to get this scratch. For others, this has to be forcibly done by doing any of the following:

a. Change our attitude of status quo and look for any opportunity to make a change
b. Put ourselves in situations where others will force us to change or make that dent. A typical example is the position of getting into a competitive situation or being surrounded by challenging people.
c. If nothing happens, force yourself, like on a typical day, and say, I am going to change something and see what happens.

Change the status quo and keep the roundness at a level which makes life worth living and making a difference in this world. Let us not be fooled that a smooth round surface is better but a certain roughness is necessary to position ourselves with a foundation that cannot be shaken by the very same factors that we intend to conquer. Good luck in seeing yourself as the purpose of life on earth!

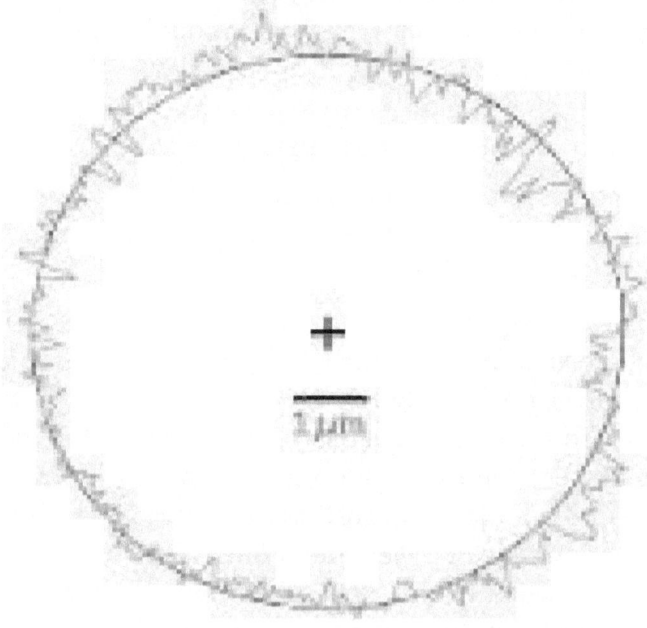

The Power of Observation

In our pursuit to be effective in whatever we do, and also to leave a mark that is positively remembered for a long time, we have to use several basic and innate capabilities we all have been bestowed with, by God. These qualities are there for everyone, but only a few polish and perfect it. Let us look at one such capability: the power of observations. Here, observations are not restricted to what we see. It also extends to what we hear, smell, feel, experience and perceive.

Observations require concentration. Another way of mentioning this is focus, which again leads to purpose and objective. In other words, the power of Observations can be cultivated if we quickly decide on some objective or purpose in different situations. If we are conducting a training session, we need to know whether the audience has accepted us or not, whether we are in sync with the audience or not, and whether we are making a mark through our program or not. This requires observations of several parameters while conducting the session, such as the audience's face, eyes, body language, what they are doing when you are talking, when you are turning, etc. This is also true when you are in conversation with someone.

Similarly, while conducting an audit, we have several parameters to observe, such as, ambient noise, temperature, enthusiasm, arrangement of files, time to retrieve records, interrupting phone calls, and so on. All these parameters are already there. What we see and interpret is called the power of observation. There are two concepts at play here: seeing and interpreting. To see, one should develop mental conditioning which can be practiced. For instance, when you have time to spare, go to the lobby of a hotel, busy road or a reception area at a client's office. Start observing the goings-on there and make note of what you see. Then, repeat this a couple of times and check whether you are seeing newer things each time. You can cultivate this art of observation with the help of a little, but focused effort.

The other aspect is to interpret. Interpretation is dependent on personal prejudices. We must, thus, learn to be very impartial and not allow what you want to interpret to overtake what the right interpretation is. You can even do this with a close friend or a colleague, and do a bit of an open analysis. You can have different types of interpretation such as negative interpretation, positive Interpretation, interpretation for a solution, interpretation to go into the root cause and so on. In general, success comes when you interpret, so that everyone will benefit and your advice ensures the success we all endeavor to get.

Sometimes, it is possible to make this a bit ambitious. This can be done by pre-empting someone's thought process by interpreting it in a manner in which the other person changes his mind. This can be done even if we had a wrong intention to begin with. For example, if you are talking to someone and you find that there is a possible negative approach. You can suddenly change the interpretation and say, "Sir, it is very nice of you to have thought about this so positively. I admire your determination to make this happen!" Even if you interpreted that he was about to cancel something, speaking this way can change things. In a way, it is like a time machine that goes backwards for a brief instant, and changes what was about to happen.

Go boldly into various situations and develop this important skill. Make others realize their goals through your power of observation. You can succeed, but making others succeed requires the right approach and an unquestionable spirit of service. Observe and Rule!

The Power of Observation

Thus Means the Mean

Here, I will take you through an interesting interpretation of the concept of Mean. All of us have heard of the Mean as a Statistical Measure and perhaps you have started wondering what you are going to visualize and learn, now. Mean comes from the world of statistics and is also called the average. In general, it represents a central tendency in a situation. For example, if you take the average of the various times at which you reach office, that number actually represents the target time you are aiming to come to office each day.

Therefore, the Mean is also called "Expectation." But, the Mean is much more than a statistic. It represents a certain philosophy, which, when understood and accepted, gives you a clear vision and attitude towards life. I will now explain this in detail. If we have several people working in a function or a group, each one performs differently. That is the truth of life. No two things are alike. There is always a variation. There are always people with good performances, and some with bad performances. But the overall performance can be summarized as the Mean performance. This is a very easy index to understand and communicate to others and to target improvements. It can also be understood as a summary capability of that group as far as performance is concerned.

Let us take this understanding a little deeper. The Mean is a central tendency somewhere in the middle, and there are some performers above and some performers below the Mean. It is so simple, but people still find it difficult to accept that all of these performers are part of the same system. Some happen to be above and some are below the Mean. People above the mean always have a tendency to look at the performers below the mean and perhaps look down upon them. Little do they realize that in a stable system, someone has to be above and someone has to be below. The people above have to support the people below, and help them upgrade themselves, thus, increasing the average. If the same people who are above the average are in a different stable system, they may well be below the average. Hence, it is always relative.

The greatest secret to learn here is that people above the average are there only because there are some people below the average.

Having accepted the fact that we will see performance and people on both of sides of the average, it is very easy to develop an attitude towards life and daily situations as follows. If a particular day has been very good for you, don't allow the ego to be inflated. Instead, start realizing that the next few days can be bad and hence, prepare yourself to accept and react in the right manner. Similarly, if a day has been bad, don't worry. The next days are yours, and you will be better off. That is the origin of hope: hope that is deeply planted in you and hope that you radiate to others around you and in your stable system so that the overall average goes up systematically. There is no place for emotion. Work sincerely, and what is due will come.

Work is worship.

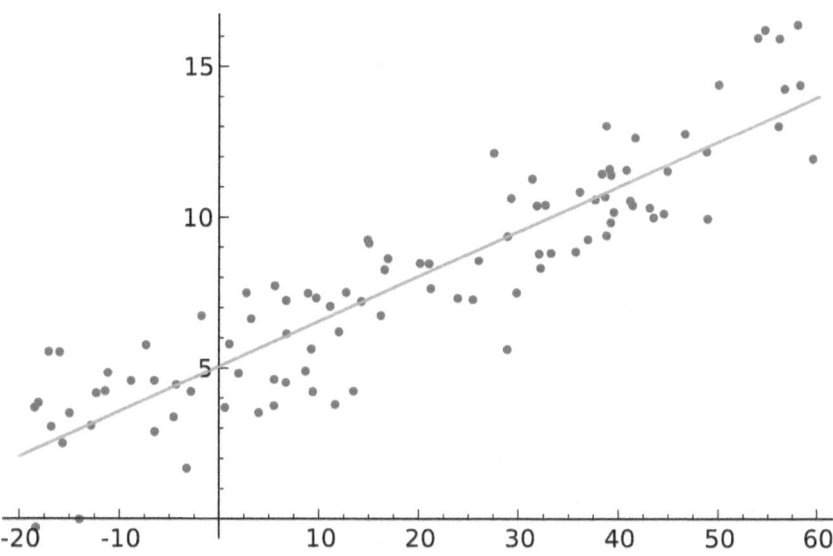

The Infinite Distance in 100 Meters

Sometimes, emotions have to be kept in check when we look at achieving overall success. What needs to be done needs to be done. We have all heard of the need for change and timeliness in making that change. Here is a story, versions of which happen in perhaps less dramatic ways around most of us.

"I lived in a small island and across the waters; I could see a bigger land. My world was so contained and resourceful. I was very happy with what I had on my small island. Once in a while, I used to hear stories of the great promise of prosperity and the future in the land across the waters. My mother always told me that long-term survival would be possible only when I would learn to cross the water. I ignored my mother as I was so confident of myself and my life and the comfort of living with her, having her shoulder to lean on, her mouth-watering food and her sheer presence with me all the time."

"But life was not to be like that, forever. Slowly the water levels rose and portions of my beautiful island were eaten away. But still, I was sure that nothing would happen. One day, my mother took me for a walk near the water and showed me the 100 meter bridge which I had to cross to be a part of a long-lasting and sustainable life. I tried to tell my mother that I would not leave her alone. She gently reminded me that going there was not for me alone, but for the good of her, also."

"Over the next few months, the water level rose further and strong winds lashed at us. But I was still wavering. One day, I saw tears in my mother's eyes. She was sobbing and I felt her pain. I decided that I would make the transition across the 100 meters bridge. I told my mother about it and she was all smiles and hugged me, and wished me all the best. I went to the bridge, but the water was very violent. There were strong winds. Many people were trying to cross and some actually managed to do so. I was just stepping on the bridge when I heard some voices talking about a few people being washed away. I did not change my mind, and took a few steps. The winds continued to lash and after about ten meters, the memory of my beautiful mother came to mind, and I did not try any further. I was back to a very disappointed mother. I told her that I would try the next day when the winds were less harsh. My mother was losing hope, but she had no choice."

"The next day, I got up to make the journey across the 100 meter bridge but there was so much resistance to face – the violent water and winds. I made a very unprepared effort to go to the bridge, but returned as the winds were stronger. The next couple of days were a mix of futile efforts, but ending with a resolve to make the transition the next day. My mother was watching me with hope and despair. One day, I woke up and thought that I would make the change, but did not even get up from the bed. By then, the water levels were closing in on my beautiful island and my mother had a weary and lost look and could only stare into space with the hope that I would make the change."

"The next day, I did not get up. I was seeing myself from outside my body. I was lying on my mother's lap and she was crying. The water was almost inside the house. I could see the disappointment in my weak mother, and still, hope that some miracle will happen. Then, there was this last lashing of wind and we all went under. We were history."

This story is meant to depict the pains involved in change. Change is something we must all make at some point in our life. Friends, the reference to the mother here is the Organization, and "I" represents the people working in the organization. The 100 meter bridge is the change – i.e., the journey – to make the company survive. The winds and violent water are the competitive forces. This is the story of many organizations which do not take the most crucial step and live in the glory of the past and are slowly forgotten. Making a change in a timely manner and in the right direction is the definition of survival.

■ I Will Make It Happen

The Opportunity to Serve and Infinite Optimism

I wish to share with you all a very important aspect of service. Many times, I have wondered which of the two is important: the opportunity to serve, or the service itself. It took me some time to confirm to myself that the opportunity to serve is most important, for two reasons:

1. It comes first
2. You have still not done the service, and therefore, there is a scope to excel

Obviously, only if our service is good, we will get more opportunities to serve. So, the opportunity to make a mark still exists if we look at the opportunity to serve with an attitude that says that one will do his best as if this is the last day of his life. How, then, should we look at the opportunity to serve? Here is a crucial message.

It is not the complete service or contract that we have for a customer which is important. We can break this into several smaller opportunities at individual levels. For Marketing, when there is a customer call, there is an opportunity to serve. Likewise, when we are making a proposal, conducting a training session, consulting, raising an invoice, talking to a customer and so on, there are infinite opportunities to serve. Take, for example, the opportunity to serve which arises when you are training people. There are several people in the audience. No one knows what the future is. Some of the people can grow to higher positions in the same company. Some others go to a different company and move to higher positions. Still others start their own businesses. Some talk about us to others and influence others. There is no end to the possibilities.

No one knows what will happen in the future. But, all I know for sure is that I am standing in the present in front of so many people whom I can influence in such a way that they benefit or cause benefits to us. So, put the burden on the Almighty and do what is right, and deliver the best you can offer in that training. There is no need to worry about the appreciation you will get. Appreciation is not the only index! You are already great as you are standing in front of so many people and making a difference to them, and definitely, a difference to you and the company in the long run. Every one there is a marketing person and several years or decades later, the benefit will accrue to each of them.

This is what you need to understand in the opportunity to serve. You can extend this logic to any service you offer, whichever position you are in, in your company, and to whom ever you offer the service. This is infinite optimism and no one can ever beat you at it. Look at each opportunity to serve with infinite optimism and do your best. The rest will follow. Success is our destiny!

Kurtosis Presides Over a Flexible Kingdom

I am a very keen student of Statistics and I have learnt a lot about life and philosophy through Statistics. The world of Statistics is a great teacher of philosophy. It depends on how we interpret various concepts and patterns that are available to us. Let us look at one such interpretation as applicable to our daily routine management. We have all learnt that data can be summarized through the four measures – Mean, Standard Deviation, Skewness and Kurtosis.

Out of all these, Kurtosis is the least used concept. In the language of statistics, it refers to the shape factor of a distribution, like, say for instance, Normal Distribution. Kurtosis represents a definition for the various shapes that can appear within the same distribution pattern. For example, for the same normal distribution, we can have several shapes such as sharp peaks, flat peaks, short peaks, tall peaks and so on. Let us leave the world of statistics here, but look at the Managerial understanding of Kurtosis. We can look at four simple shapes around the peak – the Sharp, The Flat, The Tall and the Short.

The Sharp peak refers to the management requirement of FOCUS. Focus is very essential when we are concentrating on executing a very critical activity. The Sharp peak refers to the managerial ability to stop all diversions and bring all energies into single-minded focus so that we can cut across with precision. A good manager should be capable of changing his and his team's efforts into a sharp focus, when necessary. His team should be cooperative enough to follow the leader's dictates and contribute to success in a synergetic way.

On the other hand, there are times when a Manager has to be very humble and come down from his ego and be ready to learn. This is the Short Peak of the distribution. Coming down to a level of accepting the need for learning is a key factor for learning itself. Humility and

■ I Will Make It Happen

humbleness are great qualities of a continuous learner. A manager's flexibility to come down from a position of high ego to being down-to-earth for the purpose of learning will build the internal strength to fight tougher battles.

At some other times, a Manager has to be accommodative, allowing a little extra flexibility when human relations are concerned. This is in line with taking care of people's idiosyncrasies and a bit of give and take. Here comes the Flat shape, which allows for more tolerance in attitude. A manager has to adopt this shape when required without losing control of his primary objective and that of the organization.

Righteousness and ethical behavior are the hallmarks of a good manager. They will always be relevant and strong. A manager has to stand tall under such circumstances and act like a lighthouse. The manager should radiate energy, light and warmth across a wider surrounding for which being taller than others is crucial. This is the tall peak of the distribution. Again, a manager's flexibility in becoming tall when needed is another requirement. Thus speaks Kurtosis, and gives the guidance for a good manager to assume different shapes based on the need and consequently be able to lead his team to success.

The manager should also spread Kurtosis to his colleagues so that he builds more leaders.

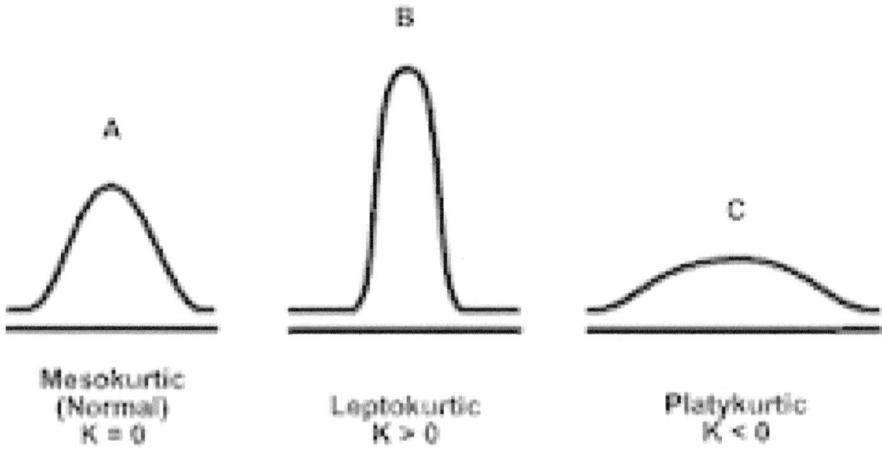

I Waited a Little More and Still, Nothing Happened

There are a lot of people who do something in their lives. There are many others who wait for something to happen without doing anything, as though the whole world is working for them and for their benefit. Ever since we have known what is what in life, we have been bitten by the bug of competition. Many people have come out with flying colors in this competition. But there are so many who have been so badly affected that they have formed a different and negative attitude and approach in life. They have all hidden under the umbrella of helplessness.

What do we do when we face competition? Adopt a helpless attitude? Join a like-minded community? Take a stand that the world is cruel and wait for something better to happen? Or, decide to take matters into our hands? Though we are sure that we have to do something, we have this approach of waiting a little more and hoping things will be better for us.

Here is the story of Mr Noname. Noname was a very shy person and did not talk even with his friends. His friends did not know what to do with him. He was baggage that went along and no serious situation built itself around him. He was one of those people who waited for something good to happen and did not make any attempt to change.

Luckily, the situation did not continue in that manner. One day, Noname decided to talk, and his friends looked at him. Slowly, his friends found that they had an additional person to talk to. Noname improved his speech and started talking about interesting things, and powerfully. His friends noticed him and gradually, he became the center of admiration and influence. His talking made him several friends: waiters at restaurants, auto drivers, even people from art and music. There was no one who did not smile after talking to him.

Noname improved himself further and started talking to large groups of people. He became a sought-after person wherever he went.

■ I Will Make It Happen

His communication abilities were recognized and people started using him to get things done and some organizations also used him as a brand ambassador for marketing. Noname realized his strength and started handling training programs, and earned in a day what others earned in a month. His fame spread and he gained more opportunities.

Noname did not stop with this. He learnt different languages, including a few foreign languages. He was able to go to other places where his friends could not even imagine going. When foreign business moved here, many people looked at this as a threat, whereas Noname looked at this as an opportunity. What Noname did was to build competitiveness, which is an internal capability and within our reach, instead of crying about competition which is external and we have no control over it.

What Noname did can be done by all of us! It need not be communication, but rather anything, in which we have interest. All that is needed is an understanding of ourselves, a serious internal development, a friendly view of this world and a strategic intent. Survival is easy for those who can do this. Competition is unknown for such people. Instead of waiting for something to happen, we can take the bull by the horns and take charge of our lives. Competitiveness is a cultivatable attribute and one which is the sole determinant of our success. Learn to be competitive and be the best in your field of interest and the world is yours!

Independent Dependence Is Always Better Than Dependent Independence

As we grow, we should become independent at least in thinking and acting. This is a source of strength for people close to us, as they know that they will not be around forever and they will depart this world with a feeling of satisfaction and fulfillment of responsibility. The same is true for any organization. When the seniors leave, they are happy that there is independence internally, and the organization will sustain itself.

The interpretation of independence for an individual is much easier as compared to an organization. When we are a year old, we struggle to stand up and our parents support us in becoming independent. As we grow and learn, we gradually cut the dependence more and more and want to be able to manage ourselves. When we start earning, the power of independence manifests in all of us. When we are actually more independent, the theory of life puts the responsibility on us to make others independent. We can understand this when we apply on our children, for instance. But, that is natural.

I will now give you a different perspective here, which is the understanding of what is unfinished. In this case, let us look at our parents. As they grow old, they are more and more dependent on us. But this dependence is generally viewed by them as weakness and it is our responsibility to make it look like they are still independent, and also to a small degree, that we are still dependent on them. That, in turn, gives them a certain feeling of power and that bonds the family powerfully. This psychology can be turned to work within an organization in a positive note. The organization has to be independent in conducting its business as far as knowledge and competence are concerned. But internally, there should be a display of dependence as this is one key parameter which builds internal bonding.

When we go to work, we are initially dependent like a child. Gradually, we build our independence till we are able to transfer independence to the next set of people. Unlike an individual, organizations are complex. Many times, a fully independent person is not respected much. Even if we are not dependent on anyone, psychologically showing dependence builds a bond and allows team work to flourish. A typical example is a boss who tells his employee, "Hi. I need support from you. I don't think I can manage this alone." This transfers a certain power to the employee and also bonds the employee to the boss and the organization.

Let us look at the truth behind this psychology. Independence and dependence also have a lot of psychological message as we will now see. In this highly complex system, there is no one who can be truly independent, but the degree of dependence has to be managed. Hence, the management of dependence is an art which can be practiced optimally.

Look at the following psychological assessment. When you are truly dependent on someone, you generally don't like it. It builds an inferiority complex in you. But, when you show dependence when you are otherwise not, builds a bond and power which integrates an organization or family. It is for the same reason that you should be able to look at the reverse, properly. For example, if you know someone is truly dependent on you, don't take advantage of this situation. Instead, make it look like that it is not so and you are only extending a little bit of support. The irony is as follows. When I am truly dependent on you, you should make it look like it is not so. When I am not truly dependent on you, I make it look like I am dependent on you to build a bond.

Team work is the essence of an organization's success. Within the organization, we should master two processes. On the one hand, we have to be independent, as true dependence is not good. But at the same time, you should show dependence even when you are not dependent, in order to build team work. When you show dependence, you are building independence in others, which is also a requirement for any organization.

Independent Dependence Is Always Better Than Dependent Independence

We have a fundamental need to be independent, though no one can be fully independent. Within an organization, we should strive to make the organization independent, even at the cost of our independence. This will come only when there is interdependence within the organization's members. If this internal dependence is true, then it is a weakness. If this dependence is managed, then it is strength. But for developing this management of dependence, we have to be fully independent. This requires a greater understanding of our strengths, our organizational needs and psychology.

Logarithms – The Profound Process Professor

Logarithms have always been a terror in the minds of students who are not mathematics-friendly. But the profundity of this concept is an eye-opener in the science of management. What does a logarithm function actually do in mathematics? It converts a multiplication or an exponential function into a series of additive functions. For instance, log (a x b) is log a plus log b and log (a power n) is n times log a which is log a added n times. I will stop the mathematics here.

The whole thing boils down to a series of additive actions. What is addition? It is a step-by-step approach when you add one experience to another, and build your total experience. The profundity is in taking one step at a time. Our mind has to think in a multiplicative manner or exponential manner. Our growth has to be exponential. Our wealth has to multiply. Our customer base has to grow exponentially. Our relationship has to multiply multifold. Our goals have to be challenging and non-linear. The impact of our actions has to reach a wide range of beneficiaries.

But, our planning has to be step-by-step. That brings us to the process. There is nothing we can achieve if we don't concentrate on the process. You can never take exponential actions or multiplicative actions. You can only act on a step-by-step basis. Maybe we take several steps at a time. Maybe we involve more people. This only increases the speed or rate of taking actions. But in the real execution sense, it is one at a time. People who have attempted several things at the same time have hardly succeeded in a sustainable manner. But people who have concentrated on taking one step at a time, but taking that action completely, have always succeeded.

The science of logarithm teaches us to concentrate on the process and specifically on how to plan. Planning is a key element of success.

Proper planning is an art that we have to master. The fundamental concept in planning is to break your total approach into a series of steps, and then assign competent resources with clear deadlines for achievement. When all these steps are integrated and executed in a coordinated manner, we get an exponential or multiplicative result.

We all have dreams and wish to grow faster. But these dreams remain unfulfilled, if we don't have a proven process to take us there. The relationship between what we want to achieve and the process we take will look like being in different planes. The mind runs faster than what we can act. That is where the function like logarithm acts as a link and teaches us to look at a step-by-step approach. Let additive but coordinated steps permeate our thinking and actions, and let us all strive to achieve goals which our minds exponentially churn out. A dream is only a dream unless it is achieved.

Rule 1 $\quad \ln xy = \ln x + \ln y$

Rule 2 $\quad \ln \dfrac{x}{y} = \ln x - \ln y$

Rule 3 $\quad \ln x^r = r \ln x$

My Daughter Becoming My Mother Is a Necessity

The logic of life ensures continuity of life through the system of transmission of genes. There are many instances where we see remarkable offspring that has all the characteristics of the people in the past. Further, the process of evolution ensures an improvement in future generations – the most significant among this being the adaptability for the requirements in the future.

Similarly, there is a need for Business Continuity. How we wish that we had a similar process of transmission of genes! Unfortunately, this is not the case as organizations have to find practical and successful ways to survive, expand, adapt and grow.

The first generation in business is characterized by passion, close contact with the customer, flexibility, learning and a lot of hard work. It is during this phase that a formula for success is created. This formula has all the genes for the business – ethics, principles, unique selling points, the chain of relationships, business priorities, the creation of a process for delivery, etc. Unfortunately, this cannot be documented in as much detail to catch the significant aspects which define success. It cannot be seen or inferred by anyone seeing it from outside, either.

Then, how does this continuity actually work? Business continuity is ensured to the second generation mostly through word of mouth and proximity with the first generation. There is a lot of danger for the loss of the precious genes from this formula for success, but there is no threat to the business as the presence of the first generation in some manner is the real contributor to success.

When the first generation fades and the third generation steps in, the Business Continuity is at the highest stage of risk. Those in the second generation who have imbibed the spirit of the first generation generally keep the fires on but they have to struggle in the wake of improper interpretations, and most importantly, the inability to adapt to the third generation. It is important to recognize that adaptability is the key success factor as the customer also undergoes this generation transformation.

Three qualities have to be recorded and transmitted in the genes or the success formula:
1. The spirit of the first generation
2. Technological business requirements which change with customer needs
3. The adaptability or the social business requirements

This will not happen unless the first generation recognizes this and transmits the knowledge to the second generation. If transmission is done through adequate efforts, the third generation is born through the second generation as a reflection of the first generation, and then, success remains assured from thereon.

Success is in the smaller details. Pay attention to every detail and infer the significance of the core value and what should change with each generation. For instance, proper communication is a core value, but how this communication is to be done is a form of adaptability. Customer Satisfaction is a core value. But what constitutes Customer Satisfaction is a form of adaptability. Let us extract the genetic factors for Business Continuity and transmit it through effective communication, so that the third generation is a reflection of the first generation.

The Problem Tells the Solution That It Is the Solution to the Problem

Many times, this question has crossed my mind. Is there a difference between the problem and solution? Let me share a perception here. I was relaxing in the sofa with my eyes closed. My mind was wandering, and I was thinking about my school days. I distinctly remember my Moral Science Teacher telling us, "Lying is a problem. Always tell the truth. That is the best solution." I was reflecting on this idea deeply, when I was suddenly brought to the present with my wife asking me, "How is this saree?" (The saree is a traditional Indian attire worn by women).

I was in a dilemma. Should I tell the truth, that the saree was no good? It was a strategy that my teacher said was good, but it would be a problem for me in the next few days. Or, should I tell her a lie, saying that the saree is excellent? That would be a problem for my teacher, but was certainly a solution for domestic peace at the time.

There are a lot of philosophers who have preached that telling a harmless lie is not a bad thing. The question is not about what is good or bad. But what is right? What is the real difference between the Problem and Solution? I once visited a customer, in my capacity as a consultant. They were discussing rejections (the Problem) and the technical people came up with "tool-breaking" as the cause.

They suggested that finding a better tool was the ideal solution. It looked technically correct. But I was wondering. Maybe tool-breaking was the solution, because by breaking, it has prevented further problems. I was reminded of the Plague in Surat, Gujarat. After the Plague, Surat has become a model city. Was Plague a problem or the Solution given by providence to clean the city? In the same way, is tool-breaking a problem or a solution? It is like the circuit tripper in the house where electrical gadgets are protected by tripping.

Experts in problem-solving will argue that we need to go to the root cause, but one can easily see that at any stage, this is a relevant question. Let us say that there is a problem in an oven. The solution is to maintain the temperature in a controlled manner. In another situation, the solution may be to clean the fixture. Are these solutions or are these problems at different levels? Maintaining temperature in a controlled manner or cleaning the fixture are good enough as problems. That is perhaps why problem-solving never sees the end of day. There are companies which have problems that they had several years ago, and they all had good solutions. But none of these were implemented in a sustainable manner – which is why I say that there is no such thing as a solution. It is also a problem. Similarly, there is no such thing as a problem. They are solutions.

The real question is not in the definition of a problem or solution. But, it is in our ability to look at it in minute detail. The ability to break up a problem or solution into minute levels so that the levels get dissolved in the working system is the right approach. It is like a tablet dissolving in water. If you break it sufficiently small it gets dissolved. Otherwise, lumps are formed.

Whether we are looking at a situation as a Problem or Solution is not important. It is most prudent to break things to many tiny steps or smaller levels, so that it is absorbed by everyone and gets into the system.

Just like we get into details while solving a problem, we should also get into equal amount of details in solving a solution. Otherwise, the solution becomes another problem.

■ I Will Make It Happen

Sigma versus Sigma – The Mature Adviser versus the Mature Analyst

Here is another thought from the world of Mathematics and Statistics. Sigma has been part of our life right from school days. Initially, we learnt addition in the world of arithmetic and learnt Sigma as an additive tool. Later, when we were introduced to the world of Statistics, we learnt about Variation and then Sigma as the Root Mean Square Deviation estimate. Now that we are in the world of Management, I wish to point out the wisdom of Sigma versus Sigma.

How do these two gentlemen position themselves in our current world of Management?

I will start with the first of these – the Additive Tool. When I think deeply, I find that Sigma does more than mere addition. Consequently, I define Sigma in the following manner: Sigma – **S**trong **I**ntegrator **G**iving **M**ature **A**dvice.

Most of us work towards targets. Each day, week or month is not the same. We have different achievements. Since we have an overall target, it makes a lot of sense to add the achievements on any "time period" basis and keep checking it against our overall target. This is the power of the cumulative. Statistics has a special name for this: the Ogive. At any time, the cumulative sum tells us how much we have to stretch and plan consequently. Many times, it is a motivator to see progress against the overall target though we have differing achievements on a comparison basis from time to time.

In a different situation, the sum total is very important for us. The cumulative years of experience, tiny bits of learning manifesting as wisdom, the integration of small efforts of a team in achieving a project objective, the tiny savings which add up sufficient money to acquire

■ I Will Make It Happen

an asset, for example, a house. As they say, tiny drops of water make an ocean. While Arithmetic Sigma is easy to understand, the Statistical gentleman is complicated even to arrive at. Let us not worry about the calculation, but concentrate on what he actually does. We can easily define Statistical Sigma in the following manner: Sigma – **S**tability **I**ndicator **G**uiding **M**ature **A**nalysis.

We also have different needs in Management, apart from addition. On one hand, it is fine to know how we fare against a target. On the other hand, we need to have control and stability in the routine "time-to-time" work life. We know that things vary. This variation should have some control first, and then, improvement. For this, we need an indicator that can be used as a base for comparison to know whether we are better off from the previous time period or not. That is where we find the importance of the second Sigma.

The beauty of this Sigma is that it is both, practical and fair. It always takes an optimized middle path, which is the best in a given situation, indicating that we start with a certain level of performance. It is fair in the sense that it gives equal importance to people performing better, and people not performing better. With such a strong indicator in hand, the Management can easily put in place efforts to improve the level of performance and also reduce the performance variation around it.

A good manager should unleash the power of this Sigma versus the Arithmetic Sigma and combine their power with the internal knowledge available and lead their team to stable and greater levels of performance and in a wise manner.

What We Have Not Understood Is Exactly What We Have To Understand

What a nice pair of words – understand and understood! To bring the proper context, let us extend it a bit further: "to understand" and "to have understood."

On the face of it, these are simple words depicting awareness, knowledge or to know. But when we look at the context of everyday life or Management, these have powerful messages. Let us start with "to understand." It shows a "before" situation. To "have understood" is an "after" situation. The irony is that what we have to understand is validated only after we demonstrate what we have understood. "To understand" is part of the planning process. "To have understood" is part of the performance.

Let us look at some real life examples. In Management, an employee comes with a proposal for an investment. The Management, knowing the current financial situation, wishes that the employee would understand that there is no resource available at present, though his idea is good. But, the employee understands differently. He thinks that the Management does not wish to invest in his project. He will demonstrate what he has understood in the form of a complaint or loose talk to others in the organization, which in turn spreads his personal bias to others.

The real difference between "to understand" and "have understood" is the emotional and internal bias which is built with years of experience.

A person who has never experienced the rewards of punctuality is conditioned by a bias which goes as follows. To be punctual is understood by the person as not having any work and being late is the right indicator of being busy. It is an assumed requirement. So, when you ask such a person to come at 9:00 AM, the interpretation is to leave his place at 9:00 AM, and not actually be available at the destination at 9:00 AM.

When you ask a person to be available at 9:00 AM, you wish that there is a certain understanding of this expectation. What the other person has understood is known only when you check the time the person actually arrives.

We preach that in Quality, we have to understand the stated and the implied needs of the customer. When a customer asks for delivery to be made on the twelfth, the expectation is the product to arrive at the customer's place on the twelfth. But, what is understood is that the product should leave around twelfth. In all these cases, there is a possibility of other factors coming in the way of our commitment. But these factors are part of the process and an understanding is not complete unless we understand the expectations of performance and the process of accomplishing it.

It is always a good practice to take the literal meaning of what is mentioned instead of interpreting it in our own way. A good or bad experience will not alter the real meaning of a need. The interpreted meaning is the real culprit. To further justify that interpretation is a crime and to stick to that interpretation is a chronic problem from which there is no salvation. We need breakthrough actions. Breaking all the barriers including past bias is the real expectation. Nothing will change when a person does not change this bias. A wise man once said, "We will not see change, if we don't change." The starting point is to define a better understanding of the word "understand" and bridge the gap between what we have to understand and what we have actually understood.

The Difference Between Sharing and Evaluation – The Visible Versus the Invisible

Many times, we are caught in a dilemma between when to share and when to evaluate. Both are powerful concepts and should be done correctly. If they are done in the wrong sequence, it defeats the glory and purpose of the concepts.

Evaluation creates the much-needed segmentation to take things forward. Sharing creates the bond between the various segments.

When you are talking about motivation, share fully. There is no need to evaluate, as the power of expression is all that is needed. The same is true when you are contributing in a brainstorming session. But, if someone asks you for advice, you have to evaluate first, before sharing. If someone talks about their personal problems, sharing is the most essential thing, and not evaluation. But, if the person is talking about his future, evaluation precedes sharing.

When you wish to do charity or give a gift, sharing is the most natural thing to do. But when you are planning to invest, evaluation is the right thing to do first.

This does not imply that we don't evaluate what we share, or don't share what we evaluate. Unless sharing and evaluation are complimentary, there is a danger of going off track. Here we are fundamentally referring to the sequence.

Let us look at these two concepts a bit closely. Sharing is emotional, spontaneous, and is dependent on the situation and to whom we are communicating. It is also visible. The other person sees the approach and the effort. It sends a signal that we are setting everything aside and giving full attention to the person involved. On the other hand, evaluation is very precise, rational and logical. It weighs the pros and cons before delivering the result. But, the process of evaluation is invisible to the receiver and can go the opposite way in communicating as the lack of interest. It is in this context that we have to determine the sequence. Remember, we have to do both. If we don't evaluate after sharing, we don't have a calibration of what is right and wrong, and of what is emotional and what is logical. If we don't share the evaluation, there is no learning for anyone.

There is no need to share everything we evaluate, as it often conveys no value and many of the outputs have great internal benefits in the form of learning. But sharing knows no boundaries. All that is needed is the radiation of openness and warmth. Eventually, emotions and logic are intertwined and make a person strong. In any given situation, we have to use the right sequence. Ultimately, the key element is to reduce the time lag between sharing and evaluation or vice versa, to such an extent that we have full control of our thoughts and communication processes that we can interchange quickly and deliver a powerful impact to the receiver.

This is a capability that is best learnt by practice and comes from a genuine interest to succeed. One has to realize that the temperament needed for sharing is totally different from the one that is needed for evaluation. At the same time, one has to be careful not to compromise on certain fundamental principles which are common to both sharing and evaluation. There should be no bias. There should be thoroughness, completeness and timeliness. The mastery of switching from one to another, as and when needed, is the supreme test of this capability.

The Difference Between Sharing and Evaluation – The Visible Versus the Invisible

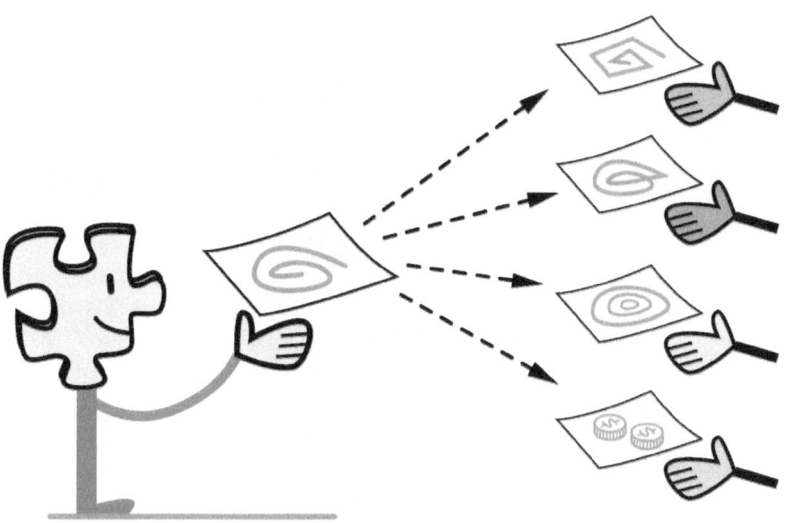

Strength Depends On Where the Weakness Lies

We all want to be strong and condemn weakness in any form. We work hard to overcome weakness. There are many situations in life where we derive strength from the most unexplained or least understood things. Let us look at this through examples.

Look at the power of a piece of steel of a few centimeters length. It is so powerful that it gives many of us the confidence and courage, and above all, the privacy. One example is the bathroom or bedroom where the few centimeters long latch is all the privacy, confidence and strength for us. In business, a document that is a few microns, and signed, with a few ounces of ink, becomes a binding contract. It has the power to regulate the mightiest of people. We can go further down and say that the mere thought of God brings a certain discipline and behavior which is accepted by everyone.

By itself, the few centimeters long steel, a few microns paper or a thought has no power and can be considered weak. Their power is derived from the position they occupy and the time at which they occupy the position. This brings me to the subject of this discussion: the position of such weak things in real life has a tremendous influence on the strongest personalities. If we analyze deeply, we will certainly come to the conclusion that strength is derived by where we place the seemingly weak things in life.

Look at another example. A strip of fabric has no strength. But, if it is placed by a person of authority on the road, it can divert traffic. A child is weak from all physical angles. But the mere thought of the child is a motivator for the existence for several people, who are otherwise facing problems. There are many words in many languages, which when placed and arranged properly, can make or break a relationship. The list goes on.

From a Management point of view, these weak things are not placed at random and do not get there by chance. We have to place them to derive strength. There is no one who is absolutely strong. We are all strong from an angle of relativity. That is why there is life, and more importantly, there is a balance in life and everyone survives in his or her own way.

Take for instance several things which by themselves do not look big, or even capable of doing anything spectacular. Commitment to do what you committed to, being punctual, telling the truth, constancy of purpose, a kind word, involvement in things and so on. Today, we know that these are things which are powerful. They are powerful, because great people like Gandhi have placed them properly and demonstrated how to derive strength. If these are placed in position and sequence properly they can conquer anything.

The reason this succeeds is the rationale of the human mind and the fact that all of us are capable of being good. We are able to perceive and interpret things, which is why we are able to connect such things and derive strength. So, friends, you are all strong and can be stronger if you are able to place things properly and in the right sequence. We are weak if we choose to be weak. We will be strong if we place ourselves and all those stand alone weakness, in the right place at the right time.

All the best!

Can We Frame the Customer?

....

I am always wondering what the future model for any company would be. We only survive if we keep adapting to changing demands and profile of the customer. As I see it, the future will witness a combination of versatility, speed and precision. The more I thought about it, the more I became clearer with the model and the FRAME model evolved, which I share with you all.

The first is "F." In the future (I see it already now), the customer will look for people and organizations who know a lot of things, and at a reasonable level – enough to keep their interest to discuss further. The customer requirements are becoming more complex. They will not have time to talk to several people. The first thing they will do is not look for new entrants. They would like to talk about their needs with known people, and only if known people show lukewarm response or lack of knowledge, they will look elsewhere. Just as we say that acquiring customers are more difficult than retaining existing ones, it is also true that acquiring new suppliers or service providers are also going to be increasingly expensive and demanding. That is the first part of the model which I call the "Funnel." If we can make a big funnel, then all the customer's needs will fall inside the funnel and at least we have a chance as the customers have talked to us. The key competence is to read and be familiar to discuss many issues at a level of interest, which is engaging to the customer and enough to place their needs in the funnel.

Then we have the "R." The needs inside the funnel will not remain there for long. It will evaporate quickly. The next level of competence is to respond to this at such a rapid pace that even lightning will feel shy. The response needs to be fast, interesting, helpful and friendly, so that customer interest is preserved and this will ensure that the needs don't evaporate, but get fixed in our relationship and expectations with the customer.

Can We Frame the Customer?

The next is "A." This should be followed by a very acceptable and user-friendly engagement model – technically supportive and commercially friendly. Make it easier for the customer to work with us. We should not give complex proposals which don't commit any deliverable within a reasonable time period and commercial terms which are easy to understand and more important – which are easy for a customer to commit immediately.

Then comes "M." Once the engagement is confirmed, we are better than anyone in the competition as we have a contract. Then, we start quickly building a mesh around the customer in all imaginable contexts. Typical examples are friendly planning, simple communication, motivating presence, understandable documentation and approach, using innovative but simple set of tools, ownership which gives comfort level to the customer and so on. In other words, the mesh arrests all degrees of freedom and the customer remains with us. This actually complements the funnel in as much as more ""needs" can get in. It is a mesh and not a concrete wall – which means we are transparent, we are open to suggestions, we involve any and all relevant partners and we are honest and truthful of success or failures.

The last is "E." Finally, success is in execution. There must be a bombardment of deliverable which covers all aspects of the customer expectations so much so that the customer is FRAME-D with us forever. The sequence of delivery is more of what the customer wants and may not be what is documented. The ability to prioritize and deliver quickly is the only challenge. This actually means a step-by-step approach for each of us to enhance our competency in small steps and in a focused manner as outlined above. None of us are going to succeed alone. It is the team which matters and the ability of the team is the sole criteria to remain and contribute. I urge each of you to analyze yourself and find gaps for your internal improvement and the fruits of this journey are awaiting us.

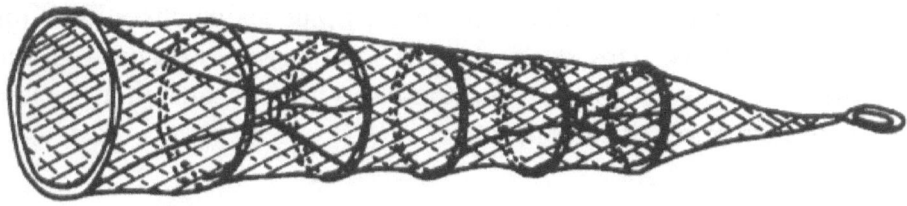

Assignable Causes Are To Be Assigned Intelligently

∙∙

In this message, we will see a new perspective for "assignable causes." We have learnt that a stable process is free from assignable causes. Alternately, assignable causes are those that prevent the process from being predictable. It is a stable process that is characterized by a bell-shaped pattern.

The significance of the bell-shaped pattern is the fact that there is a peak performance around a center, and as we move away from the center, the performance reduces towards zero. This is a very useful concept for performance and many designs are built around this concept. So far so good!

What if we don't want this kind of performance? There are quite a few situations, where we want different kinds of performance. Take the example of Sales. If you have a product range, we need sales, if possible equally or in whatever ratio we plan for, for all the products. We certainly don't want peak sales for a particular size or color or item and lower performance as the size changes. In a production system, we want equal production every day, or every hour, or as per what we plan. A teacher wants all her students to perform well, with certain unavoidable fluctuation.

Here, we are not referring to small variations, which happen regularly. For instance, we know that when there is a setting, there will be peak performances at the setting and an inherent variation around the setting. But, we want a process which ensures that we have different settings for different situations. In the examples above, it could be for students, products, sizes, days, etc. The setting should ensure that the performance is as per plan, or rectangular, which means, more or less equal performance for each situation.

That is why assignable causes are important as they determine settings. We should have control over assignable causes for either eliminating different settings to get a singular performance like in a bell-shaped pattern, or, manage assignable causes in such a way that you get different settings such that the performance is near equal or as per a plan.

We need not think that assignable causes are always a problem. They are also very useful under differing expectations. Ultimately, it is our ability to grasp the fundamental theory of an assignable cause, the causal relationships and the ability to know how to control them and control them in a manner which gives you the desired performance.

Mastery is needed so that we can introduce or eliminate assignable causes as per our desires, and to achieve a planned performance. Merely being a spectator and offering explanations is not Management. Instead of watching things happen, let us move towards getting things done.

Carpet Bombing

Carpet Bombing is a term used in war where the aggressor drops a series of bombs over the entire area. The chances of survival of those on ground are limited. The bombs are dropped from a low height so that the surface area is covered.

I am neither interested nor am I referring to war in this essay. Instead, I am looking at the power of this concept in Marketing.

Conceptually, three elements constitute Carpet Bombing, which are relevant to marketing. These are:

1. Defining an area
2. Delivering a series of bombs
3. Bombing from a low height

For a person in Marketing, and for the entire company, getting the opportunity to do business is the way to success. So, everyone in your company can be involved in this process. Let us look at the three concepts from a Marketing perspective.

Defining an area: This can be anything, starting from every company in a city or every city in a state or every state in the country or every country in the world. The limitation is only in our thinking. If we can resolve that we should be present globally, the work in front of us is not going to be over in this generation.

Delivering a series of bombs: This is the equivalent of reach. We have to be practical. We can never hope to be physically present everywhere. But, we can have people, i.e., professionals, agents, organizations, associations, networks, and such else, to be associated with us in every country or each city in every country. These people are our brand ambassadors. They will wake up each day thinking about us. To make them do this is ability in innovative thinking spiced by a commitment to deliver and a track record of such delivery.

Carpet Bombing

Bombing from a low height: If we speak from a very high level, no one will understand us. We have to go down to their level. Compatible Communication is important. When we go close to ground level, we have the chance of recognizing and bringing a huge variety of people into our world. The more the variety, the more the chances of getting opportunities from varied segments of customers. All that we have to do is to start the process of acquiring - Not only customers but getting people who can get us customers.

Let us start with a resolve. Let us say that each one will get at least one external person to be associated with us. That person's only job is to think of us when they get up each morning. Each Morning CAN be a very Good Morning for us!

Good Morning!

Learn To Unlearn. Unlearning Strengthens Our Learning

Learning and unlearning are two pillars through which we acquire knowledge. We have discussed this subject in several ways on several occasions. Still, I am amazed by the serious connections that exist between real life technological phenomena and the fundamentals of acquiring knowledge.

After I graduated and worked as a trainee, one skill I had to learn was "how to weld." It was a tough skill to acquire. The process was extremely demanding. We had to make a pass of weld deposit, then stop the welding and remove the slag by slowly hitting the weld deposited with a tool until the slag scales were removed. After each pass, we had to do this. Sometimes, we used to take short-cut due to lack of patience. Without proper slag removal, we would deposit the next weld. The result was that the joint was weak and had poor strength levels. The lesson remains etched in my mind.

Now I see the relevance of the same in the process of knowledge acquisition.

Depositing the weld is like learning new points in the knowledge gaining process. The slag removal is like unlearning. Now, I realize that learning and unlearning are not just two processes, but are connected very strongly and depend on each other for success. If slag removal is not done properly, the next weld deposit has no value. The same is true with learning and unlearning.

Unlearning has to be done seriously. It should not only remove the surface layer, but go beyond that. Scratch the surface and open up fresh pores. Once this is done, the learning process bonds well with what we already know and make it strong. Otherwise, it is like copying something from a book and then applying it without any thought or preparation. By sheer weight of communication, the new knowledge might seem useful and well-accepted. But it will just remain on the surface without a bond. With any slight force, the new deposit of knowledge will be washed out.

Those who have done training sessions will immediately recognize this. After a session, you will find some participants asking, "Sir, the session is good. But do you think it will work in India or our company?" Another may ask, "Sir, where have you done this?" These questions sometimes look like negative questions. I have assumed that there will be always such participants who consider this question as their only purpose of attending. But on introspection, I see that they are unlearning and we have to be patient with them. We need to give them proper counseling. If not, it will end up as the poor weld joint.

Let us not dismiss unlearning as a notional and cosmetic process. It has to hurt. Yes, unlearning has to hurt the layer. Then, the recipients of new knowledge are opened up and a better bond is generated, finally. It is like shaking the system. It is also equivalent to rebirth. For rebirth we have to die. Here dying is like killing the irrelevant pieces of information that are stagnating. We have to train ourselves to unlearn Learn to unlearn and then unlearn to learn!

The Teachings of Sine Theta

Building competitiveness is extremely important. However, the first step is to understand the competition and our position vis-a-vis the competition. Once you know your position, it is simple to derive the best strategy for survival. I was amused when I found a very effective way to appreciate competitive positions using Sine Theta – the Trigonometry idea.

The definition of Sine Theta is, the Opposite Side divided by Hypotenuse. Theta is an angle which can be from 0 degrees to 360 degrees. At first, it is sufficient to understand up to 90 degrees. After that, it is a question of changing the quadrant and direction. From an organization and competitive point of view, the opposite side is the competition or the most significant competitor. The Hypotenuse is the diagonal, and in a way, represents our capability across the organization.

For a market leader, the opposite side is always less than the hypotenuse and hence the angle is only between 0 degrees to 90 degrees. For a level-playing field, the angle can go up to 90 degrees, in which case you are in a market where your main competitor is almost the same as you are. If you have no significant competitor, then the angle is 0 degrees and you are in a monopoly, which is not very desirable from the point of view of a healthy market.

In a level-playing field with competitors being equal from the point of view of an "order of magnitude," various strategies adopted by key players are towards changing the angle continuously and by smaller amounts. This is to keep the market vibrant, by way of new initiatives and offerings.

If there is no level-playing field wherein your competitor is much bigger than you, then the angle is above 90 degrees. When we are in that position or wish to enter a market where there are big players, the lesson from Sine Theta is to change the position or segment. Sine 120 is

Cosine 30. Alternately, it is sine of 180 minus 60 which is still sine but with a different angle. Another way to understand this is to segment the market and offer a different position. That is what has happened – Sine has become Cosine and 120 degrees has become 30 which is equal to market segmentation.

This change of position (Sine to Cosine) and segmentation (angle and strategy) is the competitiveness which I am talking about. The basic theory is that there is no company which can be equally strong on all segments, and hence, there is always the opportunity for competing effectively. We have to be ready. Being ready is not like writing semester exams when readiness is sufficient, in time for the exam to arrive. Being ready is a continuous exercise and should be the backbone of our daily approach to business. Let us compete effectively through a combination of "Understanding ourselves" and the "Market Dynamics."

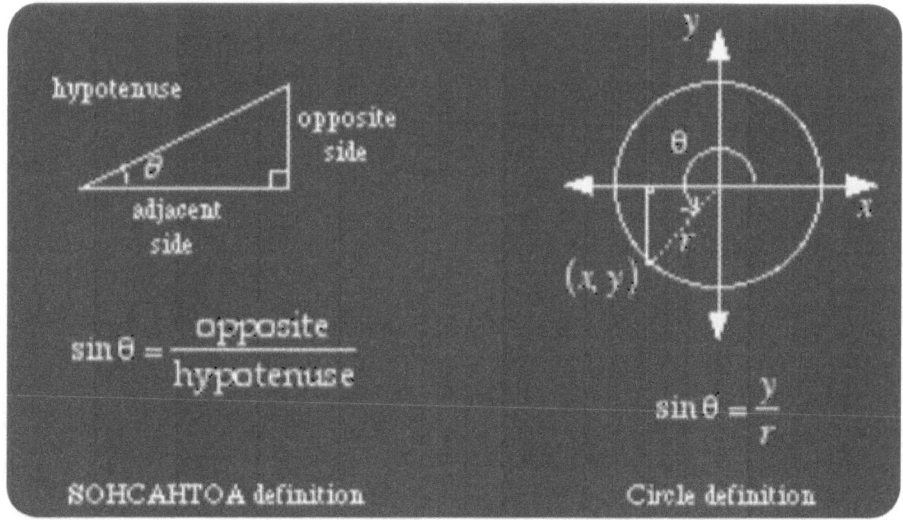

Infinite Optimism Is the Only Antidote for Eternal Uncertainty

I learnt the power of the two words, "Eternal Uncertainty," very recently. It is not something new. The two words aptly summarize what we have always been undergoing, in life. When we sit in review meetings, we see Eternal Uncertainty. Marketing, every month, reiterates that we will get our orders. It has gone to the MD's table. It is just a matter of time!

Payment: We always eagerly expect it in the hope that we will get the money that week or month. Many of us, when we know that there is uncertainty, express this as expecting the payment by the end of the month.

Look closely. The KRA (Key result Area), internal projects and skill development are all examples of Eternal Uncertainty in any organization. Except for a statement that it will happen, we have learnt to express Eternal Uncertainty in a confusing way.

There are two parts here.

One is Eternal Uncertainty due to factors outside our control.

Second is Eternal Uncertainty due to our inability or lack of will to act.

The second is a crime and should not be viewed as Eternal Uncertainty. The first reason – factors beyond our control is a challenge. But accepting that nothing can happen is a defeatist attitude. There are a few things we can do – for instance:

a. Can we minimize the impact of factors outside our control by better planning?

b. Can we find other controllable factors which can overcome the factors beyond our control? Such as, preempting the customer and being more proactive. We need not wait for the customer to say that the invoice is not there. We can find better ways for ensuring that the customer never uses that excuse.

But all this means "proactive action." If we are capable of proactive action and we put into action this concept, then there is hope. One day, we will succeed. That is Infinite Optimism. Optimism is life and hope. Infinite means full patience and never giving up. The only medicine for Eternal Uncertainty is Infinite Optimism.

With infinite optimism we can do the following:

a. We will never accept defeat and hence keep doing something
b. When things don't happen the way we want, we can quickly take corrective measures in our thinking
c. When factors "beyond control" crop up, we don't accept them, but like White Blood Corpuscles, attack the disease of uncertainty in a proactive manner

Be optimistic. But don't be foolishly optimistic – "foolishly optimistic" means waiting for the result without putting in any effort. Being intelligently or smartly optimistic means putting in well-conceived proactive actions to ensure that results will come – sooner or later.

"Maegha Sandesham" – The Message of the Clouds

In today's technology, we talk of Cloud Computing and related matters. I will speak of a simple message which the clouds have always shared with us.

When there is energy applied on water in the earth, it evaporates. On a global scale, we have clouds forming due to this. These clouds retain water in a different but pure form. There is electric charge due to the chemical structure of the water stored. The clouds move together. When certain physical conditions are attained, they discharge the water in the form of rain. It is quite possible that due to winds, the clouds sometimes move away and disintegrate and later rejoin in a different location. This is a cycle which has been going on from the time of the formation of the universe. The clouds show us that we can get pure water even from dirty or polluted water as the process of evaporation just takes the water away, leaving the sediments back where they belong.

This is a message for all of us. We were all pure when we were born. But as we grow, we gain knowledge and develop attitudes that make each of us different. Some of these attitudes, knowingly or unknowingly, do not allow us to be pure anymore. These are the sediments we acquire. After some time, the inertia is so much that we cannot move anywhere. Here, the movement is growth towards betterment of ourselves and society.

Can we remain in that state forever? Should we remain in that state forever? Clouds teach us that there is nothing permanent and we are all transient. We need to shed sediments time and again and evaporate to our pure form, retaining the original form in which we were born and the pure knowledge we acquired. In that state, we will always meet like-minded people and will travel together to a different destination and then deposit ourselves for the good of the society there.

This does not mean that we have to physically move. This only means that we attain a different state and look at the world and people around us from a different plane. This is like rebirth. For rebirth, we have to die. Here, I mean the death of wrong attitudes and unwanted burdens. When we are reborn, we are born lighter and can thus travel faster and touch the lives of more people, and be in a position to influence them.

In an organization, this means newer service offerings, which are in line with the aspiration of the people, i.e., the customers of the future. Such organizations are always alive as they are close to birth and not death. Let us imbibe the spirit of the clouds and continue the Maega Sandesham.

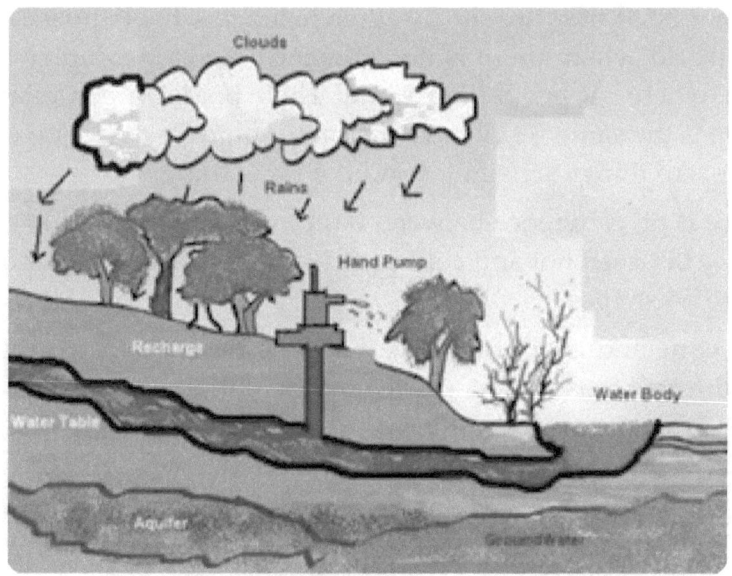

I Am It

Variation narrates its significance.

Hello. My name is Variation. Just stop for a while and KNOW me, if you can. I am one thing that is always constant. As long as the electron vibrates, I am there. In short, I am life. If I stop, then you also stop existing. A lot of people have tried to understand me and some have even measured me using fancy names like Sigma. But have you understood what I am?

I signify life and also variety. No two things are similar and they should not be. If they are similar, then listen to what happens. Do you want a world where there is no difference between people? Imagine a world where all people are same. Their bodies are similar. Their language is the same. They have the same color. There are no different creatures. All things are similar and the same thing.

There is no difference between happiness and sorrow. There is no difference between hot and cold or day and night. There are no colors. There are no shapes.

Everyone and everything has the same height and weight. There are no different seasons. There are no different times.

Wait a minute! We will never know anything and there is no identity!

Is it not the same as death? Life is awareness. The beauty in life is the variety and that is me. When things change, we notice. When we notice, we question. When we question and seek answers – we learn. I am the essence and existence of life. With me around, you enjoy life. The only way to live life happily is by accepting what is there as it is and relate it to me.

Don't question as the answer you will get is simply not right. Don't attempt to remove me as then you are moving towards death. But I allow you to control me. And control is always related to an objective.

The objective is having a short influence span and hence, it is worth controlling. Control does not mean elimination. If you try to eliminate me, you are eliminating yourself.

You are yourself because of me. Your identity is because of my existence.

I am God. The variation and spice of life.

Fighting the Process Civil War through Good Governance

In Management, we all face two types of problems

1. Sporadic
2. Chronic

Sporadic problems come once in a way. We know how to solve them as there is attention and no one is comfortable with it. Thus, it gets solved quickly. Chronic Problems, on the other hand, are always there and often taken for granted. Many times, the first challenge is to accept that there is such a problem. Typical examples are meetings always starting ten minutes late, the always found gap between plans versus actual, and such else. The best way to attack Chronic Problems is to have an organized program in the company and involving "everyone" and "every area."

In continuous improvement, the main principle is working on the inherent causes or system causes to get better levels of performance. Assignable causes are never a problem as they always manifest in some manner which can be studied and eliminated.

This is like terrorism and civil war. If there is a major uprising like a war between two countries or attacks like the USA's on Iraq and Afghanistan, it is easy to tackle them as you know from where it comes. The concentration of the entire nation or state can be channelized in that direction. But if the war is fought internally by people hiding in smaller pockets and all over the country, it will never be easy to fight this. Take Afghanistan and Iraq now. After the strike by USA, the war is now internal and it will take several years to end as people are hiding somewhere and will attack at their convenience.

India had its share of this like in Punjab and in North east and also the many internal terror strikes we are witnessing.

Let us look at why this is powerful by taking an example

Let us say you are in your house and through a small crack, you are observing the world outside. You have all the clarity as the small hole affords you a much focused view of any spot. The environment outside is totally oblivious of you and your observation. If you decide to attack, it is very easy and the outside environment has no clue and is totally unprepared.

On the other hand if you are standing in the outside world, you can never know that there is such a crack and you are being observed. Even though the outside world is rosy and enjoyable you have no safety and you are always vulnerable.

The system and inherent causes are like the people watching through cracks and the people in charge of problem-solving will have an enormous task to move into "Solving" capability. But the answer is also obvious.

Good governance with open and transparent communication of intent is enough to flush all the people hiding to come into the open and embrace the system, Likewise, a good process approach, a good housekeeping and a disciplined compliance at all levels in the process flow is enough to keep the inherent causes at a distance and at whatever power you wish them to have.

People deserve respect and they expect the same. When you abuse a person – intentionally or unintentionally and also when fairness is lost, people first move into a shell – which is the equivalent of those pockets and they observe us from there. As we continue to behave in the irrational manner, they attack.

Likewise, process parameters and all the technological features – which we call causes – deserve respect and fairness. In the name of aggression – achieving targets or showing production – if we knowingly or unknowingly abuse the process parameters, it performs the equivalent of attack when we least expect.

Just like good governance is the key to have a happy population, it is good process management and compliance at all levels which is essential to control all the complex causes which affect the process.

Just like people are educated to improve their thinking and maturity, processes must be taught to experiment to find better levels for themselves and with minimum overall waste.

Please give life to what you are doing and convey the beauty of life to everyone so that our leadership position is maintained.

Heights and Distances – The Depths of Influence

All of us have our trysts with Heights and Distances at school level, in mathematics. Let us examine their contribution to influence.

In general, the understanding of heights is anything that is above the ground, and it is hence a Vertical. Distances are generally along the ground and consequently understood as Horizontal. Though they are seen as being in different planes, their contribution together is phenomenal.

We can look at the domain of our influence on anything – people, organizations, information or knowledge, research, etc as being horizontal. In terms of the above discussion, as distance. We can have a huge coverage of distance and hence a huge domain of influence – just by being outgoing and through networking. But the real assessment of our influence is known only when we rise above. Being in the same plane, we cannot appreciate or judge the power we have as we are also part of the same system. Deming had said strongly that the real contribution to a system comes only when we look at the system from outside.

This is where Height is important. The moment we move up – here, moving up is not in the physical sense, but more in terms of positioning and the way we articulate ourselves. When we move up, we tend to see the distances and obstacles more clearly. By virtue of this, we can significantly contribute to influence and in return, the entities influenced also look at us with genuine respect.

Likewise, the beauty of a Height cannot be understood if we are very close to the object. You will never be able to see the beauty of a building from being under it. The only way we can see the beauty is when we move away from the object and move into the distance. In a way, the people being influenced are able to appreciate us only because they are at a distance and we are at a height.

It is a matter of charge, i.e., energy, which determines how much distance is good or how much height is good. There is no formula. It is only related to energy, presence, contribution and clearing the environment around – a misty confused air is not good visibility.

That brings us to the key element of this discussion – Energy or Charge. We have to constantly seek higher levels of charge and re-charge to be of any value. Charge comes from a deep motivation to achieve and an equally deep knowledge of how to achieve something. No one is born with this quality. We can get this quality when we find ourselves in a position where this quality is the essence of existence. Different people find themselves in this situation at different points of time. Some are there for shorter durations and some are there for a long haul.

Stop a bit and introspect and then analyze yourself. Find out your current domain of influence and then gradually move upward in the thought process and you will suddenly see the distance, i.e., domain of influence, becoming short.

At this point of time, all you need is respect and love for yourself and the charging process will start.

Being successful is equally important for the sustainability of the charging process. Also success is the only factor which will keep the word of mouth spreading. Hence, concentrate on being successful. This actually means planning and executing small activities which are completed successfully. Doing more small activities is better than doing a very complicated activity. The complex problems will get solved automatically when we have the ability to tackle smaller problems. But never bask in personal glory. But work through people and share success and give credit to others. Then you move up on the Height and then automatically the Distance increases.

Don't look for appreciation. Instead, teach people to appreciate themselves and they will in turn, appreciate you. This will have a dramatic impact of clearing the air of misty confusion around and it will enable people to see you at the height even when they are at a distance. Let us become good influencers and create more influencers.

Heights and Distances – The Depths of Influence

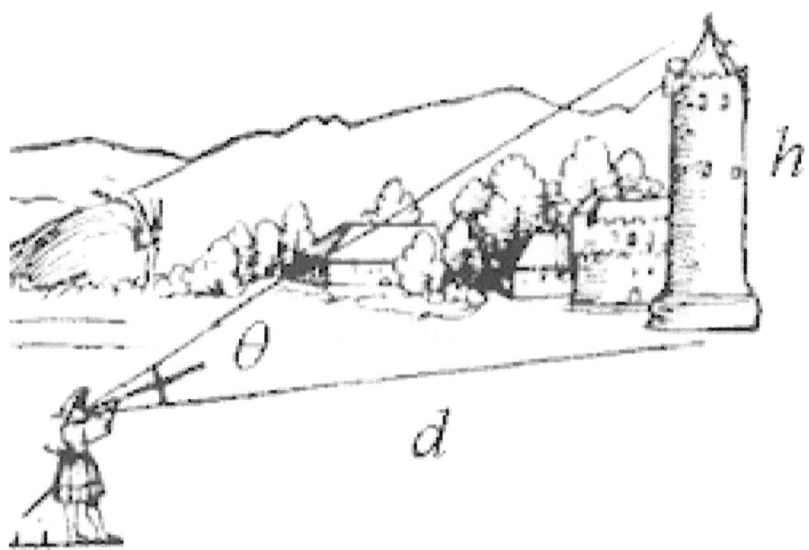

The Anamalous Behavior of the Result of Expectations

Many things in life are not linear. Many things reverse at crucial times and cause you embarrassments. We are so used to linear thinking that we make predictions without thinking about this concept of "Anomalous Behavior."

Take for instance a company which added fifty clients in a year. Immediately, they think that the next year should be fifty or more. They do quick math and come to a conclusion that they will have 500 clients in ten years as a minimum. Does this actually happen? No.

Take another example. We manage to save Rs 25,000 in a year. We then start the math and assume we will have Rs 2.5 lakhs (one lakh is same as hundred thousand) in ten years and so on. It gives us a very good feeling to think of savings in that manner. Linear thinking, but does this actually happen? No.

Except for a few rare instances, it rarely happens the way we imagine. Something or the other happens and we are forced to accept defeat. What actually happens is, a complex set of forces act on our system. Soon, we get very disappointed with the result. Why does this happen?

Start by accepting the Law of Anomalous Behavior.

Take water for example. When you cool water, it starts to reduce in volume. You keep cooling it and the water keeps reducing in volume. But at four degrees Celsius, the water starts expanding. The effect creates problems for piping systems. This law is called Anomalous Expansion of water. It is a theory in Physics.

What happens in Physics also happens in real life. The problem is in accepting it. We can easily accept linear as it is logical. We can also accept that things get flattened. But things reversing 100% is a very

The Anamalous Behavior of the Result of Expectations

surprising and embarrassing phenomenon. Why does it happen? It is complex to understand. The fact that it happens should give a mature and practical tinge to our approach to planning.

The problem is not in the law. But it is in our lack of maturity of assuming that things will continue to behave in a very predictable manner – more often a predictable way that we want to see happen.

In Cricket, we say that nothing can be concluded till the last ball is bowled. Same is true in life. We cannot and should not conclude the result of our expectations till the last activity is performed.

That is why experience comes more from execution and watching and learning from what actually happens. Of course, with the learning, we should refine our theory and then knowledge is developed. This becomes wisdom when we apply it in our next cycle planning. Anomalies and contradictions are the lifeline of research. Watching out for them and learning from them is what differentiates between flying without control and being practically grounded.

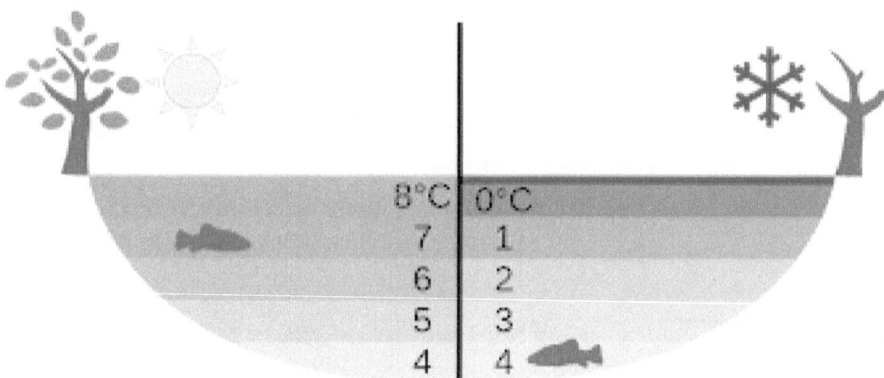